AF292196

DAWAD

AIR FRYER TOASTER OVEN COMBO

COOKBOOK FOR BEGINNERS

THE COMPLETE GUIDE OF DAWAD AIR FRYER TOASTER OVEN WITH 1000-DAY MOUTH-WATERING, FRESH AND FOOLPROOF RECIPES

DAVID LACEFIELD

CONTENTS

VEGETABLES AND VEGETARIAN **94**

DESSERTS **105**

INTRODUCTION

How the DAWAD Air Fryer Oven Works

An air fryer works by rapidly circulating hot air and a small amount of oil to fry foods. The oil and air work in tandem, transferring heat both via conduction (the direct contact of the hot oil) and convection (the heavy rotation of hot air). In a wall oven or the oven of a range with convection, the air fry function works the same way.

The Benefits of the DAWAD Air Fryer Oven

An air frying oven uses little to no oil to create a flavorful and crunchy texture on foods and boasts all of the same benefits as a standalone air fryer - with some additional conveniences.

The air fry feature is integrated right into your oven, eliminating the need to store an extra appliance or take up valuable counter space.

An air frying oven has more capacity, saving you time and allowing you to cook more food at once so that there's always enough for the whole family.

An air fry oven does more than just air fry, so one appliance works harder for you. Enjoy other features such as Even Baking with True Convection, Fast Steam Cleaning, and Smudge-Proof Stainless Steel.

The Preparations for the DAWAD Air Fryer Oven

1. Find the right place for your air fryer oven in your kitchen. Make sure you have some clearance around the oven so that the hot air can escape from the vent at the back.
2. Preheat your air fryer before adding your food. Because an air fryer heats up so quickly, it isn't critical to wait for the oven to preheat before putting food inside, but it's a good habit to get into. Sometimes a recipe requires a hot start and putting food into a less than hot oven will give you less than perfect results. For instance, pastry bakes better if cold pastry is placed into a hot oven. Pizza dough works better with a burst of heat at the beginning of baking. It only takes a few minutes to preheat the oven, so unless you're in a real rush, just wait to put your food inside.
3. Invest in a kitchen spray bottle. Spraying oil on the food is easier than drizzling or brushing, and allows you to use less oil overall. It will be worth it!
4. Think about lining your drip tray with aluminum foil for easy clean up.

How to Clean Your DAWAD Air Fryer Oven

After we have all the basic knowledge about the air fryer toaster ovens, let's discuss the very common question; how to clean a Cuisinart convection toaster oven, or how to clean a convection toaster oven? Following is a list of ways to clean it:

Clean it with homemade dish soap cleaner

For the best and safe cleaning, it is necessary to unplug your toaster oven and disconnect the apparatus from the force source before you start cleaning.

Also, obviously, never inundate it in water. After that, put the toaster oven on a bit of paper to get the pieces, then take out the metal plate, rack, and lower scrap plate and spot them in the sink. Then, use dish soap and water to wash these parts.

To battle any difficult stains on these removable pieces, and let them dry totally while you clean the remainder of the machine.

The next step is to make your own cleaning answer for the inside of the toaster oven by consolidating vinegar, warm water, and a little dish soap. Apply that to the inside with a clammy wipe.

However, do whatever it takes not to get any of the fluid on the warming components. Some toaster ovens have a porcelain polish or a nonstick inside that makes them marginally simpler to clean.

In any case, it very well may be harmed by metal scouring cushions and rough cleaners. You can utilize a wipe, material, or old cloth when cleaning down your toaster oven.

Clean it with baking soda

You might get surprised to know that how to clean a toaster oven with baking soda. Let us tell you the process in detail:

Baking Soda is incredible for cleaning since its normally antacid nature artificially responds to water and vinegar, which makes dirt and oil break down rapidly and without any problem.

Baking soda is an all-common substance present in every living thing. While the vast majority know it for baking, it's properties are extraordinary for a wide assortment of things.

It likewise has an incredible rough quality if not weakened excessively, so it's an extraordinary option in contrast to other markets since baking soda is an incredibly protected and powerful cleaning item.

Also, baking soda is totally non-poisonous and protected to use around food, children, and pets. You can also clean the heating component in your toaster oven by utilizing a gentle soap and a clean, buildup free cloth on a cool, unplugged toaster oven.

Tenderly wipe the loops guaranteeing no buildup from the cleaning cloth remains. Also, it is normal to have water and soap on the cloth; however, try not to get the radiator component significantly wet.

However, if we don't clear every ounce of buildup off, you'll get that delightful toasted baking soda smell whenever you use it. For another, we would prefer not to chance to harm the component, driving you to purchase another one.

Therefore, keep in mind that we have to unplug the toaster oven and do nothing until it's totally cool. Then, take a wipe or material in some warm water. Then start delicately cleaning the length of the warming component to and fro.

If you're following our entire how to clean a toaster oven with baking soda steps, this should be the first thing you do. As we said toward the beginning, try not to utilize soap or different cleaners on the warming components as they could harm it.

Try to let everything dry first prior to stopping the toaster oven back in or utilizing it. To clean a toaster oven with baking soda, make a glue with baking soda and water. In a cool, unplugged toaster oven, spread the glue within the oven, dodging the warming components.

Let it sit for 12 hours or more. For minor cleaning, 1 hour should do the trick, and then wipe clean with a soggy fabric and warm water. After that, we are well aware of the cleaning methods; let us understand the best way to turn off the digital air fryer.

BREAKFAST

Baked Curried Fruit

Servings: 4
Cooking Time: 25 Minutes

Ingredients:

- Curry mixture:
- 2 tablespoons dry white wine
- 1 teaspoon lemon juice
- ¼ teaspoon ground allspice
- ¼ teaspoon ground ginger
- ¼ teaspoon ground cardamom
- ¼ teaspoon turmeric
- ¼ teaspoon ground cumin
- ¼ teaspoon ground coriander
- Pinch of grated nutmeg
- Pinch of cayenne
- 2 tablespoons honey
- 1 teaspoon soy sauce
- 1 16-ounce can pear halves, drained
- 1 8-ounce can pineapple chunks, drained
- 1 16-ounce can peach halves

Directions:

1. Preheat the toaster oven to 350° F.
2. Combine the curry mixture ingredients in a 1-quart 8½ × 8½ × 4-inch ovenproof baking dish and add the fruit, mixing well.
3. BAKE, uncovered, for 25 minutes, or until bubbling and the sauce is thickened. Cool and serve on a sesame wafer with Creamy Yogurt Sauce.

Beef And Bean Quesadillas

Servings: 2

Cooking Time: 30 Minutes

Ingredients:

- Quesadilla filling:
- 1 8-ounce flank steak, trimmed and cut into thin ⅛ × 2-inch strips
- 1 jalapeño pepper, seeded and minced
- 2 plum tomatoes, chopped
- 1 small onion, cut into thin strips
- 1 bell pepper, seeded and cut into thin strips
- 2 garlic cloves, minced
- 1 15-ounce can black beans, rinsed and drained
- 2 tablespoons chopped fresh cilantro
- ½ cup reduced-fat Monterey Jack cheese
- 4 6-inch flour tortillas
- Low-fat or fat-free sour cream

Directions:

1. Combine the filling ingredients in an oiled or nonstick 8½ × 8½ × 2-inch square baking (cake) pan, mixing well to blend.

2. BROIL for 10 minutes, remove from the oven, and turn the pieces with tongs. Broil for 10 minutes, or until the pepper, onion, and beef are cooked and tender. Remove from the oven and transfer to a bowl. Add the beans and cilantro and mix well.

3. Spread one quarter of the tortilla mixture in the center of each tortilla. Sprinkle each tortilla with 2 tablespoons cheese. Roll up the edges and lay each, seam side down, in the pan.

4. BROIL for 10 minutes, or until the tortillas are lightly browned and the cheese is melted. Serve with sour cream.

Creamy Bacon + Almond Crostini

Servings: 20
Cooking Time: 10 Minutes

Ingredients:

- 1 baguette loaf, cut into ½-inch-thick slices
- 2 tablespoons olive oil
- 4 ounces cream cheese, cut into cubes, softened
- ½ cup mayonnaise
- 1 cup shredded fontina cheese or Monterey Jack cheese
- 4 slices bacon, cooked until crisp and crumbled
- 1 green onion, white and green portions, finely chopped
- ¼ teaspoon Sriracha or hot sauce
- Dash kosher salt
- ¼ cup sliced almonds, toasted
- Minced fresh flat-leaf (Italian) parsley

Directions:

1. Toast the slices of the baguette in the toaster oven.
2. Arrange the toasted baguette slices on a 12-inch pizza pan or a 12 x 12-inch baking pan. Lightly brush the slices with the olive oil.
3. Preheat the toaster oven to 375°F.
4. Beat the cream cheese and mayonnaise in a medium bowl with an electric mixer at medium speed until creamy and smooth. Stir in the fontina, bacon, green onion, Sriracha, and salt and blend until combined.
5. Distribute the cheese mixture evenly over the toasted bread. Top with the sliced almonds. Bake for 6 to 8 minutes or until the cheese is hot and beginning to melt. Allow to cool for 1 to 2 minutes, then garnish with minced parsley. Serve warm.

Apple Maple Pudding

Servings: 4
Cooking Time: 20 Minutes

Ingredients:

- Pudding mixture:
- 2 eggs
- ½ cup brown sugar
- 4 tablespoons maple syrup
- 3 tablespoons unbleached flour
- 1 teaspoon baking powder
- 1 teaspoon vanilla extract
- ¼ cup chopped raisins
- ¼ cup chopped walnuts
- 2 medium apples, peeled and chopped

Directions:

1. Preheat the toaster oven to 350° F.
2. Combine the pudding mixture ingredients in a medium bowl, beating the eggs, sugar, and maple syrup together first, then adding the flour, baking powder, and vanilla. Add the raisins, nuts, and apples and mix thoroughly. Pour into an oiled or nonstick 8½ × 8½ × 2-inch square baking (cake) pan.
3. BAKE for 20 minutes, or until a toothpick inserted in the center comes out clean.
4. BROIL for 5 minutes, or until the top is lightly browned.

Good Stuff Bread

Servings: 2
Cooking Time: 40 Minutes

Ingredients:

- First mixture:
- 1 apple, peeled and grated
- 1 carrot, peeled and grated
- 1 cup unbleached flour
- 2 teaspoons baking powder
- ⅓ cup chopped walnuts
- ⅓ cup raisins
- ⅓ cup rolled oats
- ⅓ cup shredded sweetened coconut
- Blending mixture:
- 1 banana
- 1 egg
- 1 cup low-fat buttermilk
- 2 tablespoons dark brown sugar
- 2 tablespoons vegetable oil
- Salt to taste

Directions:

1. Preheat the toaster oven to 375° F.
2. Combine all the first mixture ingredients in a medium bowl and stir to mix well. Set aside.
3. Process all the blending mixture ingredients in a blender or food processor until the mixture is smooth. Add to the first mixture ingredients and stir to mix thoroughly. Transfer to an oiled or nonstick 8½ × 4½ × 2¼-inch regular size loaf pan.
4. BAKE for 40 minutes, or until a toothpick inserted in the center comes out clean and the top is well browned.

Hot Italian-style Sub

Servings:3
Cooking Time: 15 Minutes

Ingredients:

- 3 Italian-style hoagie rolls
- 3 tablespoons unsalted butter, softened
- 1 teaspoon Italian seasoning
- ½ teaspoon garlic powder
- 9 slices salami
- 12 slices pepperoni
- 3 thin slices ham
- 3 tablespoons giardiniera mix, chopped
- 6 tablespoons shredded mozzarella cheese

Directions:

1. Preheat the toaster oven to 350°F. Split the rolls lengthwise, cutting almost but not quite though the roll. Place the sandwiches in a 12 x 12-inch baking pan, side by side with the open side face up.
2. Combine the butter, Italian seasoning, and garlic powder in a small bowl. Spread evenly on the inside of the hoagie rolls.
3. Layer a third of the salami, pepperoni, and ham on each sandwich. Sprinkle with the giardiniera mix and mozzarella cheese.
4. Bake for 10 to 15 minutes or until heated through and the cheese is melted.

Baked Eggs With Bacon-tomato Sauce

Servings: 1

Cooking Time: 12 Minutes

Ingredients:

- 1 teaspoon olive oil
- 2 tablespoons finely chopped onion
- 1 teaspoon chopped fresh oregano
- pinch crushed red pepper flakes
- 1 (14-ounce) can crushed or diced tomatoes
- salt and freshly ground black pepper
- 2 slices of bacon, chopped
- 2 large eggs
- ¼ cup grated Cheddar cheese
- fresh parsley, chopped

Directions:

1. Start by making the tomato sauce. Preheat a medium saucepan over medium heat on the stovetop. Add the olive oil and sauté the onion, oregano and pepper flakes for 5 minutes. Add the tomatoes and bring to a simmer. Season with salt and freshly ground black pepper and simmer for 10 minutes.

2. Meanwhile, preheat the toaster oven to 400°F and pour a little water into the bottom of the air fryer oven. (This will help prevent the grease that drips into the bottom drawer from burning and smoking.) Place the bacon in the air fryer oven and air-fry at 400°F for 5 minutes.

3. When the bacon is almost crispy, remove it to a paper-towel lined plate and rinse out the air fryer oven, draining away the bacon grease.

4. Transfer the tomato sauce to a shallow 7-inch pie dish. Crack the eggs on top of the sauce and scatter the cooked bacon back on top. Season with salt and freshly ground black pepper and transfer the pie dish into the air fryer oven. You can use an aluminum foil sling to help with this by taking a long piece of aluminum foil, folding it in half lengthwise twice until it is roughly 26-inches by 3-inches. Place this under the pie dish and hold the ends of the foil to move the pie dish in and out of the air fryer oven. Tuck the ends of the foil beside the pie dish while it cooks in the air fryer oven.

5. Air-fry at 400°F for 5 minutes, or until the eggs are almost cooked to your liking. Sprinkle cheese on top and air-fry for an additional 2 minutes. When the cheese has melted, remove the pie dish from the air fryer oven, sprinkle with a little chopped parsley and let the eggs cool for a few minutes – just enough time to toast some buttered bread in your air fryer oven!

Buttermilk Pancakes

Servings: 4
Cooking Time: 20 Minutes

Ingredients:

- Batter:
- 1 cup low-fat buttermilk
- 1 egg
- 1 cup unbleached flour
- 3 tablespoons wheat germ
- 1 tablespoon honey
- 1 tablespoon olive oil
- Salt to taste
- 1 teaspoon baking powder
- 1 tablespoon olive oil for brushing pan
- Honey, maple syrup, or molasses

Directions:

1. Blend the batter ingredients in a food processor or blender until smooth. Stir in the baking powder. Pour enough batter into an oiled or nonstick 9½-inch-diameter round cake pan to make the size pancake you prefer.
2. BROIL 5 minutes, or until the batter pulls away from the sides and starts browning. Remove the pan from the oven and, with a spatula, turn the pancake over.
3. BROIL again for 5 minutes, or until the pancake is lightly browned. Transfer to a plate and repeat the broiling steps for the remaining batter. Serve with honey, maple syrup, or molasses.

Hashbrown Potatoes Lyonnaise

Servings: 4
Cooking Time: 33 Minutes

Ingredients:

- 1 Vidalia (or other sweet) onion, sliced
- 1 teaspoon butter, melted
- 1 teaspoon brown sugar
- 2 large russet potatoes (about 1 pound), sliced ½-inch thick
- 1 tablespoon vegetable oil
- salt and freshly ground black pepper

Directions:

1. Preheat the toaster oven to 370°F.
2. Toss the sliced onions, melted butter and brown sugar together in the air fryer oven. Air-fry for 8 minutes, help the onions cook evenly.
3. While the onions are cooking, bring a 3-quart saucepan of salted water to a boil on the stovetop. Par-cook the potatoes in boiling water for 3 minutes. Drain the potatoes and pat them dry with a clean kitchen towel.
4. Add the potatoes to the onions in the air fryer oven and drizzle with vegetable oil. Toss to coat the potatoes with the oil and season with salt and freshly ground black pepper.
5. Increase the air fryer oven temperature to 400°F and air-fry for 22 minutes tossing the vegetables a few times during the cooking time to help the potatoes brown evenly. Season to taste again with salt and freshly ground black pepper and serve warm.

Cherry Almond Scones

Servings: 12
Cooking Time: 25 Minutes

Ingredients:

- 2 3/4 cups all-purpose flour
- 1/2 cup sugar
- 1 tablespoon baking powder
- 3/4 teaspoon salt
- 1 cup dried cherries
- 1 cup slivered almonds
- 1/2 cup cold butter, sliced into tablespoons
- 2 large eggs
- 1/2 cup sour cream
- 1 teaspoon almond extract
- 1/2 teaspoon vanilla extract
- 1 tablespoon milk
- Coarse sugar

Directions:

1. Preheat the toaster oven to 375°F.
2. In a large mixer bowl, stir flour, sugar, baking powder and salt until blended.
3. Add butter pieces. Beat on MEDIUM speed until mixture is crumbly with some larger pieces of butter.
4. In a large mixer bowl on MEDIUM-HIGH speed, beat eggs, sour cream, almond extract and vanilla extract until blended.
5. Stir into flour mixture until mixture is blended and no longer dry. Lightly knead in cherries and almonds.
6. Divide dough in half. Form each into circles about 3/4-inch thick on parchment-lined baking sheet.
7. Brush each circle with milk and sprinkle tops with coarse sugar. Using a floured metal spatula, cut each circle into 6 wedges. Separate the wedges, leaving 1/2-inch between each wedge.
8. Bake for 20 to 25 minutes or until golden brown. Cool for 15 minutes before serving.

Zucchini Melt

Servings: 6
Cooking Time: 16 Minutes

Ingredients:

- Sandwich mixture:
- 1 small zucchini, chopped
- 1 plum tomato, chopped
- 2 tablespoons chopped scallions
- ¼ cup sliced mushrooms
- 1 bell pepper, seeded and chopped
- 1 tablespoon olive oil
- 2 tablespoons minced pimientos
- 1 teaspoon dried oregano
- ½ teaspoon dried basil
- 1 teaspoon minced garlic
- 6 slices multigrain or rye bread
- ½ cup shredded low-fat mozzarella cheese
- 2 tablespoons grated Parmesan cheese

Directions:

1. Combine the sandwich mixture ingredients in a medium bowl, mixing well.
2. Transfer to an oiled or nonstick 8½ × 8½ × 2-inch square baking (cake) pan.
3. BROIL for 10 minutes, or until the zucchini and scallions are tender.
4. Spoon the mixture onto each slice of bread in equal portions. Sprinkle each slice with equal portions of the cheeses. Place the bread slices on a broiling rack with a pan underneath.
5. BROIL for 6 minutes, or until the cheese is melted.

Rosemary Bread

Servings: 6
Cooking Time: 15 Minutes

Ingredients:

- Spread:
- 3 tablespoons olive oil
- 2 tablespoons margarine
- 1 teaspoon garlic
- 2 tablespoons grated Parmesan cheese
- 3 1 tablespoon finely chopped fresh rosemary leaves
- ½ teaspoon freshly ground black pepper
- Salt to taste
- 1 French baguette, sliced 2 inches thick

Directions:

1. Preheat the toaster oven to 350° F.
2. Combine the spread ingredients in a small bowl, blending well with a fork. Adjust the seasonings to taste.
3. Spread the mixture on both sides of the bread slices and wrap the loaf in aluminum foil.
4. BAKE for 10 minutes. Remove from the oven and peel back the foil, exposing the top of the bread loaf. Bake for another 5 minutes, or until the top is lightly browned.

Breakfast Banana Bread

Servings: 6

Cooking Time: 40 Minutes

Ingredients:

- 2 ripe bananas
- 1 egg
- ½ cup skim milk
- 2 tablespoons honey
- 1 tablespoon vegetable oil
- 1 cup unbleached flour
- ¾ cup chopped trail mix
- 1 teaspoon baking powder
- Salt

Directions:

1. Preheat the toaster oven to 400° F.
2. Process the bananas, egg, milk, honey, and oil in a blender or food processor until smooth and transfer to a mixing bowl.
3. Add the flour and trail mix, stirring to mix well. Add the baking powder and stir just enough to blend it into the batter. Add salt to taste. Pour the mixture into an oiled or nonstick 4½ × 8½ × 2¼-inch loaf pan.
4. BAKE for 40 minutes, or until a toothpick inserted in the center comes out clean.

Baked Eggs And Bacon

Servings: 2

Cooking Time: 25 Minutes

Ingredients:

- 8 slices bacon
- 4 large eggs
- 2 teaspoons fresh chives or scallion greens, chopped
- Sea salt, for seasoning
- Freshly ground black pepper, for seasoning

Directions:

1. Place the baking tray on position 1 and preheat the toaster oven on BAKE to 400°F for 5 minutes.
2. Arrange the bacon slices in four (4-ounce) ramekins, 2 per cup. Overlap the slices over the bottom and sides so that as much of the cup is covered as possible.
3. Bake for 10 to 15 minutes. The fat will start to render, and the bacon will start to crisp and brown on the edges. Take the ramekins out of the oven and lightly blot any excess oil in the bottom of each one.
4. Crack 1 egg into each cup, sprinkle with chives, and season lightly with salt and pepper.
5. Bake for 10 minutes, or until the egg yolks reach the desired consistency.
6. Take them out of the oven and run a knife around the edge of each cup to loosen and remove from the ramekin. Serve.

Roasted Vegetable Frittata

Servings: 1
Cooking Time: 19 Minutes

Ingredients:
- ½ red or green bell pepper, cut into ½-inch chunks
- 4 button mushrooms, sliced
- ½ cup diced zucchini
- ½ teaspoon chopped fresh oregano or thyme
- 1 teaspoon olive oil
- 3 eggs, beaten
- ½ cup grated Cheddar cheese
- salt and freshly ground black pepper, to taste
- 1 teaspoon butter
- 1 teaspoon chopped fresh parsley

Directions:
1. Preheat the toaster oven to 400°F.
2. Toss the peppers, mushrooms, zucchini and oregano with the olive oil and air-fry for 6 minutes, redistribute the ingredients once or twice during the cooking process.
3. While the vegetables are cooking, beat the eggs well in a bowl, stir in the Cheddar cheese and season with salt and freshly ground black pepper. Add the air-fried vegetables to this bowl when they have finished cooking.
4. Place a 6- or 7-inch non-stick metal cake pan into the air fryer oven with the butter using an aluminum sling to lower the pan into the air fryer oven. (Fold a piece of aluminum foil into a strip about 2-inches wide by 24-inches long.) Air-fry for 1 minute at 380°F to melt the butter. Remove the cake pan and rotate the pan to distribute the butter and grease the pan. Pour the egg mixture into the cake pan and return the pan to the air fryer oven, using the aluminum sling.
5. Air-fry at 380°F for 12 minutes, or until the frittata has puffed up and is lightly browned. Let the frittata sit in the air fryer oven for 5 minutes to cool to an edible temperature and set up. Remove the cake pan from the air fryer oven, sprinkle with parsley and serve immediately.

Crepes

Servings: 6

Cooking Time: 27 Minutes

Ingredients:

- ½ cup unbleached flour
- ¾ cup skim milk
- 1 egg
- 2 teaspoons vegetable oil
- Salt to taste

Directions:

1. Whisk together all the ingredients in a small bowl until smooth. Set aside.

2. Preheat an oiled or nonstick 9¾-inch round pie pan by placing it under the broiler for 2 minutes, or until the pan is heated but not smoking. Remove from the oven and spoon 2 tablespoons crepe batter into the pan, tilting the pan to spread the batter evenly into a circle. Return to the broiler.

3. BROIL for 4 minutes, or until the crepe is cooked but not browned. Remove the pan from the oven and invert onto paper towels to cool and drain. Repeat the procedure with the remaining batter.

Breakfast Pizza

Servings: 2

Cooking Time: 60 Minutes

Ingredients:

- 3 tablespoons extra-virgin olive oil, divided, plus extra for drizzling
- 1 recipe Classic Pizza Dough (recipe follows), room temperature
- 4 ounces whole-milk mozzarella cheese, shredded (1 cup)
- ½ ounce Parmesan cheese, grated (¼ cup)
- 2 ounces (¼ cup) cottage cheese
- ⅛ teaspoon dried oregano
- 4 ounces breakfast sausage, casings removed
- 4 large eggs
- ⅛ teaspoon table salt
- ⅛ teaspoon pepper
- 2 tablespoons minced fresh chive

Directions:

1. Coat small rimmed baking sheet with 2 tablespoons oil. Press and roll dough into 11 by 8-inch rectangle on lightly floured counter. (If dough springs back during rolling, let rest for 10 minutes before rolling again.) Transfer dough to prepared sheet and re-stretch dough into 11 by 8-inch rectangle. Brush dough evenly with 1 teaspoon oil and cover with plastic wrap. Let sit in warm spot until slightly risen, about 20 minutes.

2. Adjust toaster oven rack to lowest position and preheat the toaster oven to 450 degrees. Remove plastic and, using your fingers, make indentations all over dough. Bake until dough has puffed slightly, 5 to 7 minutes.

3. Combine mozzarella and Parmesan in bowl. Combine cottage cheese, oregano, and remaining 2 teaspoons oil in separate bowl.

4. Remove sheet from oven and, using spatula, press down on any air bubbles. Spread cottage cheese mixture evenly over top, leaving ½-inch border around edges. Pinch sausage into dime-size pieces and arrange evenly over cottage cheese mixture. Sprinkle mozzarella mixture evenly over pizza, leaving ½-inch border. Using back of spoon, create 4 evenly spaced indentations in cheese, each about 3 inches in diameter. Crack 1 egg into each well, then sprinkle with salt and pepper.

5. Bake until crust is golden brown on bottom and eggs are just set, 9 to 10 minutes for slightly runny yolks or 11 to 12 minutes for soft but set yolks. Remove pizza from pan and transfer to wire rack; let rest for 5 minutes. Sprinkle with chives and drizzle with extra oil. Cut into 8 equal pieces and serve.

Chili Cheese Cornbread

Servings: 4

Cooking Time: 20 Minutes

Ingredients:

- Nonstick cooking spray
- ¾ cup yellow cornmeal
- ¾ cup all-purpose flour
- ¼ cup sugar
- 1 ¾ teaspoons baking powder
- ½ teaspoon baking soda
- ½ teaspoon table salt
- ½ teaspoon chili powder
- ½ cup sour cream
- ½ cup buttermilk
- 2 large eggs
- 3 tablespoons unsalted butter, melted and cooled slightly
- 1 tablespoon canola or vegetable oil
- 1 ¼cups shredded sharp cheddar cheese
- 1 cup frozen corn, partially thawed
- 1 (4-ounce) can chopped green chilies

Directions:

1. Preheat the toaster oven to 425°F. Spray a 9-inch round cake pan with nonstick cooking spray.
2. Whisk the cornmeal, flour, sugar, baking powder, baking soda, salt, and chili powder in a large bowl.
3. Whisk the sour cream, buttermilk, eggs, melted butter, and oil in a small bowl. Pour the wet ingredients into the dry ingredients and stir until completely combined. Stir in the cheese, corn, and green chilies.
4. Pour the batter into the prepared pan. Bake for 15 to 20 minutes, or until a wooden pick inserted into the center comes out clean. Let cool for 5 minutes. Cut into wedges and serve warm.

LUNCH AND DINNER

Parmesan Artichoke Pizza

Servings: 6

Cooking Time: 15 Minutes

Ingredients:

- CRUST
- ¾ cup warm water (110°F)
- 1 ½ teaspoons active dry yeast
- ¼ teaspoon sugar
- 1 tablespoon olive oil
- 1 teaspoon table salt
- ⅓ cup whole wheat flour
- 1 ½ to 1 ⅔ cups bread flour
- TOPPINGS
- 2 tablespoons olive oil
- 1 teaspoon Italian seasoning
- 1 clove garlic, minced
- ½ cup whole milk ricotta cheese, at room temperature
- ⅔ cup drained, chopped marinated artichokes
- ¼ cup chopped red onion
- 3 tablespoons minced fresh basil
- ½ cup shredded Parmesan cheese
- ⅓ cup shredded mozzarella cheese

Directions:

1. Make the Crust: Place the warm water, yeast, and sugar in a large mixing bowl for a stand mixer. Stir, then let stand for 3 to 5 minutes or until bubbly.

2. Stir in the olive oil, salt, whole wheat flour, and 1 ½ cups bread flour. If the dough is too sticky, stir in an additional 1 to 2 tablespoons bread flour. Beat with the flat (paddle) beater at medium-speed for 5 minutes (or knead by hand for 5 to 7 minutes or until the dough is smooth and elastic). Place in a greased large bowl, turn the dough over, cover with a clean towel, and let stand for 30 to 45 minutes, or until starting to rise.

3. Stir the olive oil, Italian seasoning, and garlic in a small bowl; set aside.

4. Preheat the toaster oven to 450°F. Place a 12-inch pizza pan in the toaster oven while it is preheating.

5. Turn the dough onto a lightly floured surface and pull or roll the dough to make a 12-inch circle. Carefully transfer the crust to the hot pan.

6. Brush the olive oil mixture over the crust. Spread the ricotta evenly over the crust. Top with the artichokes, red onions, fresh basil, Parmesan, and mozzarella. Bake for 13 to 15 minutes, or until the crust is golden brown and the cheese is melted. Let stand for 5 minutes before cutting.

Moroccan Couscous

Servings: 4

Cooking Time: 22 Minutes

Ingredients:

- 1 cup couscous
- 2 tablespoons finely chopped scallion
- 2 tablespoons finely chopped bell pepper
- 1 plum tomato, finely chopped
- 2 tablespoons chopped pitted black olives
- 1 tablespoon olive oil
- ¼ teaspoon ground cumin
- ¼ teaspoon ground cinnamon
- ¼ teaspoon turmeric Pinch of cayenne
- Salt and freshly ground black pepper to taste

Directions:

1. Preheat the toaster oven to 400° F.

2. Combine all the ingredients with ¼ cups water in a 1-quart 8½ × 8½ × 4-inch ovenproof baking dish. Adjust the seasonings to taste. Cover with aluminum foil.

3. BAKE, covered, for 12 minutes. Remove from the heat and fluff with a fork. Cover again and let stand for 10 minutes. Fluff once more before serving.

Baked Picnic Pinto Beans

Servings: 4

Cooking Time: 40 Minutes

Ingredients:

- 1 tomato, peeled and finely chopped
- 2 15-ounce cans pinto beans, drained
- 6 lean turkey bacon strips, cooked, drained, and crumbled
- 1 cup good-quality dark beer or ale
- 3 tablespoons finely chopped onion
- 1 tablespoon ketchup
- 2 tablespoons molasses
- 1 teaspoon Dijon mustard
- 1 teaspoon Worcestershire sauce
- 1 teaspoon garlic powder
- Salt and butcher's pepper to taste

Directions:

1. Preheat the toaster oven to 375° F.

2. Peel the tomato by immersing it in boiling water for 1 minute. Remove with tongs and when cool enough to handle, pull the skin away with a sharp paring knife. Chop and place in a 1-quart 8½ × 8½ × 4-inch ovenproof baking dish. Add all the other ingredients, stirring to mix well. Adjust the seasonings to taste. Cover with aluminum foil.

3. BAKE, covered, for 40 minutes.

Kashaburgers

Servings: 4
Cooking Time: 50 Minutes

Ingredients:

- 1 cup kasha
- 2 tablespoons minced onion or scallions
- 1 tablespoon minced garlic
- ½ cup multigrain bread crumbs
- 1 egg
- ¼ teaspoon paprika
- ½ teaspoon chili powder
- ¼ teaspoon sesame oil
- 1 tablespoon vegetable oil
- Salt and freshly ground black pepper to taste

Directions:

1. Preheat the toaster oven to 400° F.
2. Combine 2 cups water and the kasha in a 1-quart 8½ × 8½ × 4-inch ovenproof baking dish.
3. BAKE, uncovered, for 30 minutes, or until the grains are cooked. Remove from the oven and add all the other ingredients, stirring to mix well. When the mixture is cooled, shape into 4 to 6 patties and place on a rack with a broiling pan underneath.
4. BROIL for 20 minutes, turn with a spatula, then broil for another 10 minutes, or until browned.

Pesto Pizza

Servings: 1
Cooking Time: 20 Minutes

Ingredients:

- Topping:
- ½ cup chopped fresh basil
- 1 tablespoon pine nuts (pignoli)
- 1 tablespoon olive oil
- 2 tablespoons shredded Parmesan cheese
- 1 garlic clove, minced
- ½ teaspoon dried oregano or 1 tablespoon chopped fresh oregano
- 1 plum tomato, chopped
- Salt and pepper to taste
- 1 9-inch ready-made pizza crust
- 2 tablespoons shredded low-fat mozzarella

Directions:

1. Preheat the toaster oven to 375° F.
2. Combine the topping ingredients in a small bowl.
3. Process the mixture in a blender or food processor until smooth. Spread the mixture on the pizza crust, then sprinkle with the mozzarella cheese. Place the pizza crust on the toaster oven rack.
4. BAKE for 20 minutes, or until the cheese is melted and the crust is brown.

Chicken Gumbo

Servings: 4
Cooking Time: 40 Minutes

Ingredients:

- 2 skinless, boneless chicken breast halves, cut into 1-inch cubes
- ½ cup dry red wine
- 1 small onion, finely chopped
- 1 celery stalk, finely chopped
- 2 plum tomatoes, chopped
- 3 1 bell pepper, chopped
- 1 tablespoon minced fresh garlic
- 2 okra pods, stemmed, seeded, and finely chopped 1 bay leaf
- ½ teaspoon hot sauce
- ½ teaspoon dried thyme
- Salt and freshly ground black pepper to taste

Directions:

1. Preheat the toaster oven to 400° F.
2. Combine all the ingredients in a 1-quart 8½ × 8½ × 4-inch ovenproof baking dish. Adjust the seasonings to taste. Cover with aluminum foil.
3. BAKE, covered, for 40 minutes, or until the onion, pepper, and celery are tender. Discard the bay leaf before serving.

Healthy Southwest Stuffed Peppers

Servings: 6
Cooking Time: 30 Minutes

Ingredients:

- 1 tablespoon oil
- 1 small onion, chopped
- 1 garlic clove, minced
- 1/2 pound ground turkey
- 1/2 cup drained black beans
- 1/2 cup whole kernel corn
- 1 jar (16 oz.) medium salsa, divided
- 1/2 cup cooked white rice
- 1/2 teaspoon chili powder
- 1/2 teaspoon salt
- 1/4 teaspoon ground cumin
- 1/4 teaspoon black pepper
- 3 medium peppers, halved lengthwise leaving stem on, seeded
- 1/3 cup shredded Monterey Jack cheese, divided
- Sour cream
- Chopped fresh cilantro

Directions:

1. Preheat the toaster oven to 350°F. Spray baking pan with nonstick cooking spray.
2. In a large skillet over medium-high, heat oil. Add onion and garlic, cook for 2 to 3 minutes.
3. Add turkey to skillet, cook, stirring frequently, for 6 to 8 minutes or until turkey is cooked through.
4. Stir black beans, corn, 1/2 cup salsa, rice, chili powder, salt, cumin and pepper into turkey mixture.
5. Fill each pepper half with turkey mixture, dividing mixture evenly among peppers.
6. Top each pepper half with remaining salsa.
7. Bake 20 minutes. Sprinkle with cheese and bake an additional 10 minutes or until heated through.
8. Top with sour cream and cilantro.

Sheet Pan Loaded Nachos

Servings: 4
Cooking Time: 13 Minutes

Ingredients:

- 1 tablespoon canola or vegetable oil
- ½ pound lean ground beef
- ½ cup chopped onion
- 2 cloves garlic, minced
- 1 teaspoon chili powder
- ½ teaspoon ground cumin
- Kosher salt and freshly ground black pepper
- 6 ounces tortilla chips
- ½ cup canned black beans, rinsed and drained
- 1 ½ cups shredded sharp cheddar cheese or Mexican blend cheese
- ½ cup salsa
- Optional toppings: sliced jalapeño peppers, chopped bell peppers, sliced ripe olives, chopped tomatoes, minced fresh cilantro, sour cream, chopped avocado, guacamole, or chopped onion.

Directions:

1. Preheat the toaster oven to 400°F. Line a 12 x 12-inch baking pan with nonstick aluminum foil. (Or if lining the pan with regular foil, spray it with nonstick cooking spray.)
2. Heat the oil in a large skillet over medium-high heat. Add the ground beef and onion and cook, stirring frequently, until the beef is almost done. Add the garlic, chili powder, cumin, season with salt and pepper, and cook, stirring frequently, until the beef is fully cooked; drain.
3. Arrange the tortilla chips in an even layer in the prepared pan. Top with the beef-onion mixture, then top with the beans. Bake, uncovered, for 6 to 8 minutes. Top with the cheese and bake for 5 minutes more, or until the cheese is melted.
4. Drizzle with the salsa. Top as desired with any of the various toppings.

Crunchy Baked Chicken Tenders

Servings: 3-4
Cooking Time: 18 Minutes

Ingredients:

- 2/3 cup seasoned panko breadcrumbs
- 2/3 cup cheese crackers, crushed
- 2 teaspoons melted butter
- 2 large eggs, beaten
- Salt and pepper
- 1 1/2 pounds chicken tenders
- Barbecue sauce

Directions:

1. Preheat the toaster oven to 450°F. Spray the toaster oven baking pan with nonstick cooking spray.
2. In medium bowl, combine breadcrumbs, cheese cracker crumbs and butter.
3. In another medium bowl, mix eggs, salt and pepper.
4. Dip chicken tenders in eggs and dredge in breadcrumb mixture.
5. Place on pan.
6. Bake for 15 to 18 minutes, turning once. Serve with barbecue sauce for dipping.

Individual Chicken Pot Pies

Servings: 4

Cooking Time: 25 Minutes

Ingredients:

- 3 tablespoons unsalted butter
- ½ medium onion, chopped
- 1 carrot, chopped
- 1 stalk celery, chopped
- 1 ¼ cups sliced button or white mushrooms
- 2 tablespoons all-purpose flour
- 1 ¼ cups whole milk
- 1 tablespoon fresh lemon juice
- ½ teaspoon dried thyme leaves
- Kosher salt and freshly ground black pepper
- 1 ½ cups chopped cooked chicken
- ½ cup frozen peas
- Nonstick cooking spray
- 1 sheet frozen puff pastry, about 9 inches square, thawed (½ of a 17.3-ounce package)
- 1 large egg

Directions:

1. Melt the butter in a large skillet over medium-high heat. Add the onion, carrot, and celery and cook, stirring frequently, for 3 minutes. Add the mushrooms and cook, stirring frequently, for 7 to 10 minutes or until the liquid has evaporated. Blend in the flour and cook, stirring for 1 minute. (Be sure all of the flour is blended into the butter and vegetables.) Gradually stir in the milk. Cook, stirring constantly, until the mixture bubbles and thickens. Stir in the lemon juice and thyme and season with salt and pepper. Stir in the chicken and peas. Remove from the heat and set aside.

2. Preheat the toaster oven to 375°F. Spray 4 (8-ounce) oven-safe ramekins with nonstick cooking spray.

3. Roll the puff pastry out on a lightly floured board, to make an even 10-inch square. Cut the pastry into circles using a 4-inch cutter.

4. Spoon a heaping ¾ cup of filling into each prepared ramekin. Place a puff pastry circle on top of each and crimp the edges to seal to the ramekin. Using the tip of a paring knife, cut 3 slits in each crust to allow steam to escape. Whisk the egg with 1 tablespoon water in a small bowl. Brush the egg mixture over the top of the crust.

5. Bake for 20 to 25 minutes, or until the crust is golden brown. Remove from the oven and let stand for 5 minutes before serving.

Individual Baked Eggplant Parmesan

Servings: 5

Cooking Time: 55 Minutes

Ingredients:

- 1 medium eggplant, cut into 1/2-inch thick slices
- 1 1/2 teaspoons salt
- 1 cup Slow Cooker Marinara Sauce
- 1 package (8 oz.) fresh mozzarella, cut into 8 slices, divided
- 1 package (0.75 oz.) fresh basil, leaves only, divided
- 1/4 cup grated Parmesan cheese, divided

Directions:

1. Sprinkle eggplant with salt and place in a colander to drain for 1 hour.

2. Preheat the toaster oven to 375°F. Spray baking pan and 5 (4-inch) ramekins with nonstick cooking spray.

3. Rinse eggplant thoroughly with water to remove salt. Press each slice between paper towels to remove extra water and salt. Place on papertowels to dry. Arrange a single layer of eggplant slices in baking pan.

4. Bake 25 to 30 minutes or until eggplant is tender. Remove slices to cooking rack. Repeat baking remaining eggplant. Reduce oven temperature to 350°F.

5. In each ramekin, layer 1 slice eggplant, 1 tablespoon sauce, 1 slice mozzarella, 1 basil leaf, 1 additional tablespoon sauce and sprinkle with Parmesan cheese. Repeat layers ending with a sprinkle of Parmesan cheese.

6. Bake 20 to 25 minutes or until cheese is melted and eggplant layers are heated through.

Herbal Summer Casserole

Servings: 4
Cooking Time: 45 Minutes

Ingredients:

- 4 small yellow (summer) squashes, cut into ¾-inch slices
- 1 green bell pepper, seeded and chopped
- 1 tablespoon roasted garlic, mashed in 1 tablespoon olive oil
- ¼ cup seasoned bread crumbs
- ¼ cup grated Parmesan cheese
- ¼ cup chopped fresh parsley
- 2 tablespoons chopped fresh cilantro
- 2 tablespoons chopped onion
- 2 plum tomatoes, chopped
- 2 carrots, peeled and cut into ¼-inch slices
- 4 tablespoons fresh lemon juice
- ½ teaspoon caraway seeds
- ¼ teaspoon celery seed
- Salt and freshly ground black pepper to taste

Directions:

1. Preheat the toaster oven to 400° F.
2. Combine all the ingredients in a 1-quart 8½ × 8½ × 4-inch ovenproof baking dish, mixing well. Cover the dish with aluminum foil.
3. BAKE, covered, for 45 minutes, or until the vegetables are tender.

Spanish Rice

Servings: 4
Cooking Time: 45 Minutes

Ingredients:

- ¾ cup rice
- 2 tablespoons dry white wine
- 3 tablespoons olive oil
- 1 15-ounce can whole tomatoes
- ¼ cup thinly sliced onions
- 3 tablespoons chopped fresh cilantro
- 4 ½ cup chopped bell pepper
- 5 2 bay leaves
- Salt and a pinch of red pepper flakes to taste

Directions:

1. Preheat the toaster oven to 375° F.
2. Combine all the ingredients with 1 cup water in a 1-quart 8½ × 8½ × 4-inch ovenproof baking dish and adjust the seasonings. Cover with aluminum foil.
3. BAKE, covered, for 45 minutes, or until the rice is cooked, removing the cover after 30 minutes.

Oven-baked Rice

Servings: 2

Cooking Time: 40 Minutes

Ingredients:

- ¼ cup regular rice (not parboiled or precooked)
- Seasonings:
- 1 tablespoon olive oil
- 1 teaspoon dried parsley or
- 1 tablespoon chopped fresh parsley
- 1 teaspoon garlic powder or roasted garlic
- Salt and freshly ground black pepper to taste

Directions:

1. Preheat the toaster oven to 400° F.

2. Combine ¼ cups water and the rice in a 1-quart 8½ × 8½ × 4-inch ovenproof baking dish. Stir well to blend. Cover with aluminum foil.

3. BAKE, covered, for 30 minutes, or until the rice is almost cooked. Add the seasonings, fluff with a fork to combine the seasonings well, then let the rice sit, covered, for 10 minutes. Fluff once more before serving.

Connecticut Garden Chowder

Servings: 4

Cooking Time: 60 Minutes

Ingredients:

- Soup:
- ½ cup peeled and shredded potato
- ½ cup shredded carrot
- ½ cup shredded celery 2 plum tomatoes, chopped
- 1 small zucchini, shredded
- 2 bay leaves
- ¼ teaspoon sage
- 1 teaspoon garlic powder
- Salt and butcher's pepper to taste
- Chowder base:
- 2 tablespoons reduced-fat cream cheese, at room temperature
- ½ cup fat-free half-and-half
- 2 tablespoons unbleached flour
- 2 tablespoons chopped fresh parsley

Directions:

1. Preheat the toaster oven to 375° F.

2. Combine the soup ingredients in a 1-quart 8½ × 8½ × 4-inch ovenproof baking dish, mixing well. Adjust the seasonings to taste.

3. BAKE, covered, for 40 minutes, or until the vegetables are tender.

4. Whisk the chowder mixture ingredients together until smooth. Add the mixture to the cooked soup ingredients and stir well to blend.

5. BAKE, uncovered for 20 minutes, or until the stock is thickened. Ladle the soup into individual soup bowls and garnish with the parsley.

Fresh Herb Veggie Pizza

Servings: 4

Cooking Time: 25 Minutes

Ingredients:

- 1 9-inch ready-made pizza crust
- 1 tablespoon olive oil
- 1 4-ounce can tomato paste
- 2 tablespoons shredded part-skim mozzarella
- 2 tablespoons grated Parmesan cheese
- 2 tablespoons crumbled feta cheese
- ½ bell pepper, chopped
- 1 tablespoon chopped fresh parsley
- 1 tablespoon chopped fresh oregano
- 1 tablespoon chopped fresh basil
- ½ teaspoon red pepper flakes
- Salt and freshly ground black pepper to taste
- Pizza mixture:
- 2 garlic cloves, minced
- 1 plum tomato, chopped

Directions:

1. Preheat the toaster oven to 400° F.
2. Brush the pizza crust with olive oil and spread the tomato paste evenly to cover.
3. Combine the ingredients for the pizza mixture and spread evenly on top of the tomato paste layer. Sprinkle the cheeses over all and season to taste. Place the pizza on the toaster oven rack.
4. BAKE for 25 minutes, or until the vegetables are cooked and the cheese is melted.

Maple Bacon

Servings: 6

Cooking Time: 16 Minutes

Ingredients:

- 12 slices bacon
- ½ cup packed dark brown sugar
- 2 tablespoons maple syrup
- 1 teaspoon Dijon mustard
- 2 tablespoons red or white wine

Directions:

1. Preheat the toaster oven to 350°F. Line a 12 x 12-inch baking pan with aluminum foil.
2. Place 6 bacon strips on the prepared pan, leaving space between the strips. Bake for 10 minutes or until the bacon is almost crisp. Carefully drain the bacon and return it to the pan.
3. Combine the brown sugar, maple syrup, mustard, and wine in a small bowl. Blend until smooth. Brush the glaze over the bacon. Bake for 8 minutes. Turn the bacon and brush with the glaze. Continue to bake for an additional 6 to 8 minutes, or until golden brown.
4. Repeat with the remaining bacon strips.

Tomato Bisque

Servings: 4

Cooking Time: 25 Minutes

Ingredients:

- 1 8-ounce can tomato sauce
- 1 7-ounce jar diced pimientos, drained
- 1 tablespoon finely chopped onion
- 2 cups low-fat buttermilk
- 1 cup fat-free half-and-half
- 1 tablespoon low-fat cream cheese
- 1 teaspoon garlic powder
- ½ teaspoon paprika
- ½ teaspoon ground bay leaf
- 1 teaspoon hot sauce (optional)
- Salt and white pepper to taste
- 2 tablespoons minced fresh basil leaves

Directions:

1. Preheat the toaster oven to 350° F.

2. Process all the ingredients except the basil in a blender or food processor until smooth. Pour into a 1-quart 8½ × 8½ × 4-inch ovenproof baking dish. Adjust the seasonings to taste.

3. BAKE, covered, for 25 minutes. Ladle into small soup bowls and garnish each with fresh basil leaves before serving.

Meat Lovers Pan Pizza

Servings: 9

Cooking Time: 15 Minutes

Ingredients:

- Dough
- ¾ cup plus 1½ tablespoons warm water, 100°-110°F
- 1¾ teaspoons instant yeast
- 2 cups all-purpose flour, plus more for dusting
- 1 teaspoon kosher salt
- 1 tablespoon extra virgin olive oil, plus more for drizzling
- Toppings
- 6 tablespoons pizza sauce
- 8 ounces shredded low-moisture mozzarella
- Pepperoni slices
- 8 ounces cooked Italian sausage
- Crushed red pepper, for sprinkling
- Dried oregano, for sprinkling
- Black pepper, for sprinkling

Directions:

1. Pour water into a large mixing bowl, then whisk in the yeast. Allow to bloom for 10 minutes.
2. Add the flour and salt and mix with your hands until no dry flour remains.
3. Cover the dough tightly with plastic wrap and allow to rest at room temperature for 15 hours.
4. Add the olive oil and form into a ball.
5. Drizzle extra-virgin olive oil generously on the food tray and use your hands to coat evenly.
6. Place the dough on the food tray and spread it out slightly toward the corners of the pan.
7. Drizzle some more extra-virgin olive oil on top and use your hands to evenly coat the top of the dough.
8. Cover the dough and allow it to rest for 90 minutes.
9. Spread the dough out further so that it covers the bottom of the pan, then pop any bubbles that formed in the dough.
10. Spread pizza sauce on the dough, followed by cheese, then pepperoni and sausage.
11. Sprinkle the pizza with crushed red pepper, dried oregano, and black pepper.
12. Preheat the toaster Oven to 450°F.
13. Insert the pizza at low position in the preheated oven.
14. Select the Pizza function, adjust time to 15 minutes, and press Start/Pause.
15. Remove when done and allow to rest for 5 minutes before cutting.
16. Cut the pizza into squares and serve.

SNACKS APPETIZERS AND SIDES

Fried Mozzarella Sticks

Servings: 7

Cooking Time: 5 Minutes

Ingredients:

- 7 1-ounce string cheese sticks, unwrapped
- ½ cup All-purpose flour or tapioca flour
- 2 Large egg(s), well beaten
- 2¼ cups Seasoned Italian-style dried bread crumbs (gluten-free, if a concern)
- Olive oil spray

Directions:

1. Unwrap the string cheese and place the pieces in the freezer for 20 minutes (but not longer, or they will be too frozen to soften in the time given in the air fryer oven).

2. Preheat the toaster oven to 400°F.

3. Set up and fill three shallow soup plates or small pie plates on your counter: one for the flour, one for the egg(s), and one for the bread crumbs.

4. Dip a piece of cold string cheese in the flour until well coated (keep the others in the freezer). Gently tap off any excess flour, then set the stick in the egg(s). Roll it around to coat, let any excess egg mixture slip back into the rest, and set the stick in the bread crumbs. Gently roll it around to coat it evenly, even the ends. Now dip it back in the egg(s), then again in the bread crumbs, rolling it to coat well and evenly. Set the stick aside on a cutting board and coat the remaining pieces of string cheese in the same way.

5. Lightly coat the sticks all over with olive oil spray. Place them in the air fryer oven in one layer and air-fry undisturbed for 5 minutes, or until golden brown and crisp.

6. Remove from the machine and cool for 5 minutes. Use a nonstick-safe spatula to transfer the mozzarella sticks to a serving platter. Serve hot.

Stuffed Baby Bella Caps

Servings: 16

Cooking Time: 12 Minutes

Ingredients:

- 16 fresh, small Baby Bella mushrooms
- 2 green onions
- 4 ounces mozzarella cheese
- ½ cup diced ham
- 2 tablespoons breadcrumbs
- ½ teaspoon garlic powder
- ¼ teaspoon ground oregano
- ¼ teaspoon ground black pepper
- 1 to 2 teaspoons olive oil

Directions:

1. Remove stems and wash mushroom caps.
2. Cut green onions and cheese in small pieces and place in food processor.
3. Add ham, breadcrumbs, garlic powder, oregano, and pepper and mince ingredients.
4. With food processor running, dribble in just enough olive oil to make a thick paste.
5. Divide stuffing among mushroom caps and pack down lightly.
6. Place stuffed mushrooms in air fryer oven in single layer and air-fry at 390°F for 12 minutes or until tops are golden brown and mushrooms are tender.
7. Repeat step 6 to cook remaining mushrooms.

Smoked Gouda Bacon Macaroni And Cheese

Servings: 10-12

Cooking Time: 30 Minutes

Ingredients:
- 1 (4 oz.) French baguette, torn
- 6 slices cooked bacon, chopped
- 1/4 cup loosely packed parsley
- 2 Tablespoons butter, melted
- 1 package (16 oz.) corkscrew or elbow pasta
- 1/3 cup butter
- 1/4 cup flour
- 4 cups milk
- 1 package (8 oz.) extra sharp Cheddar cheese, shredded
- 1 package (8 oz.) smoked Gouda cheese, shredded
- 2 1/2 teaspoons Creole seasoning

Directions:
1. Preheat the toaster oven to 400°F.
2. Using S-blade with food processor running, drop bread, 1/2 of the bacon and parsley into food chute. Process until finely chopped. Gradually add melted butter; process until crumbs form. Set aside.
3. Cook pasta according to package directions for al dente. Drain and rinse with cold water. Set aside.
4. Melt 1/3 cup butter in Dutch oven over medium-high heat. Gradually add flour, whisking until smooth, about 1 minute. Slowly add milk, stirring 8 to 10 minutes until mixture is thickened and smooth. Remove from heat.
5. Stir in cheeses, remaining bacon and Creole seasoning until cheese is melted. Fold in pasta.
6. Pour mixture into 11x7-inch baking dish sprayed with nonstick cooking spray. Sprinkle with breadcrumb mixture.
7. Bake 25 to 30 minutes or until crumbs are browned and mixture is heated through.

Cranberry Pecan Rice Pilaf

Servings: 8
Cooking Time: 75 Minutes

Ingredients:

- Nonstick cooking spray
- 2 tablespoons unsalted butter
- 1 shallot, chopped
- ⅔ cup long-grain brown rice, rinsed and drained
- ¼ cup chopped pecans
- 1 (14.5-ounce) can reduced-sodium chicken broth
- ½ cup dried sweetened cranberries
- 2 tablespoons minced fresh flat-leaf (Italian) parsley
- 1 tablespoon minced fresh rosemary leaves or 1 teaspoon dried rosemary leaves, crumbled
- Kosher salt and freshly ground black pepper

Directions:

1. Preheat the toaster oven to 375°F. Spray a 2-quart casserole with nonstick cooking spray.
2. Melt the butter in a large skillet over medium-high heat. Add the shallot and cook, stirring frequently, for 3 minutes. Stir in the rice and cook, stirring frequently, until the rice is beginning to toast. Stir in the pecans and cook until the rice is golden brown and the pecans are toasted. Stir in the broth and ⅓ cup water. Heat until it just begins to boil. Remove from the heat and stir in the cranberries, parsley, and rosemary. Season with salt and pepper. Spoon the rice mixture into the prepared casserole dish.
3. Cover and bake for 70 to 75 minutes or until the rice is tender.

Sage Butter Roasted Butternut Squash With Pepitas

Servings: 4
Cooking Time: 20 Minutes

Ingredients:

- Nonstick cooking spray
- 1 medium butternut squash, peeled
- 2 tablespoons unsalted butter, melted
- 2 tablespoons minced fresh sage, plus more leaves for garnish (optional)
- 1 teaspoon honey
- ¼ cup shelled pumpkin seeds, or pepitas
- Kosher salt and freshly ground black pepper

Directions:

1. Preheat the toaster oven to 375°F. Spray a 12 x 12-inch baking pan with nonstick cooking spray.
2. Cut the squash crosswise into ¾-inch slices. Use a teaspoon to remove the seeds, as needed, from the center of the slices. Arrange the slices in a single layer on the baking sheet.
3. Stir the butter, sage, honey, and pumpkin seeds in a small bowl. Season with salt and pepper. Spoon the butter mixture over the squash slices, then brush to coat each slice of squash evenly.
4. Roast for 20 minutes or until the squash is tender. Transfer to a serving platter and spoon the seeds and any drippings over the squash. Garnish with extra sage leaves, if desired.

Savory Sausage Balls

Servings: 10
Cooking Time: 8 Minutes

Ingredients:

- 2 cups all-purpose flour
- 1 tablespoon baking powder
- ½ teaspoon garlic powder
- ¼ teaspoon onion powder
- ½ teaspoon salt
- 3 tablespoons milk
- 2½ cups grated pepper jack cheese
- 1 pound fresh sausage, casing removed

Directions:

1. Preheat the toaster oven to 370°F.
2. In a large bowl, whisk together the flour, baking powder, garlic powder, onion powder, and salt. Add in the milk, grated cheese, and sausage.
3. Using a tablespoon, scoop out the sausage and roll it between your hands to form a rounded ball. You should end up with approximately 32 balls. Place them in the air fryer oven in a single layer and working in batches as necessary.
4. Air-fry for 8 minutes, or until the outer coating turns light brown.
5. Carefully remove, repeating with the remaining sausage balls.

Cinnamon Pita Chips

Servings: 4
Cooking Time: 6 Minutes

Ingredients:

- 2 tablespoons sugar
- 2 teaspoons cinnamon
- 2 whole 6-inch pitas, whole grain or white
- oil for misting or cooking spray

Directions:

1. Mix sugar and cinnamon together.
2. Cut each pita in half and each half into 4 wedges. Break apart each wedge at the fold.
3. Mist one side of pita wedges with oil or cooking spray. Sprinkle them all with half of the cinnamon sugar.
4. Turn the wedges over, mist the other side with oil or cooking spray, and sprinkle with the remaining cinnamon sugar.
5. Place pita wedges in air fryer oven and air-fry at 330°F for 2 minutes.
6. Cook 2 more minutes. If needed cook 2 more minutes, until crisp. Watch carefully because at this point they will cook very quickly.

Cherry Chipotle Bbq Chicken Wings

Servings: 2

Cooking Time: 12 Minutes

Ingredients:

- 1 teaspoon smoked paprika
- ½ teaspoon dry mustard powder
- 1 teaspoon dried oregano
- 1 teaspoon dried thyme
- ½ teaspoon chili powder
- 1 teaspoon salt
- 2 pounds chicken wings
- vegetable oil or spray
- salt and freshly ground black pepper
- 1 to 2 tablespoons chopped chipotle peppers in adobo sauce
- ⅓ cup cherry preserves ¼ cup tomato ketchup

Directions:

1. Combine the first six ingredients in a large bowl. Prepare the chicken wings by cutting off the wing tips and discarding (or freezing for chicken stock). Divide the drumettes from the win-gettes by cutting through the joint. Place the chicken wing pieces in the bowl with the spice mix. Toss or shake well to coat.

2. Preheat the toaster oven to 400°F.

3. Spray the wings lightly with the vegetable oil and air-fry the wings in two batches for 10 minutes per batch. When both batches are done, toss all the wings back into the air fryer oven for another 2 minutes to heat through and finish cooking.

4. While the wings are air-frying, combine the chopped chipotle peppers, cherry preserves and ketchup in a bowl.

5. Remove the wings from the air fryer oven, toss them in the cherry chipotle BBQ sauce and serve with napkins!

Quick And Easy Nachos

Servings: 2

Cooking Time: 30 Minutes

Ingredients:

- 2 tomatoes, cored and chopped
- ¼ cup finely chopped red onion
- 1 tablespoon lime juice, plus lime wedges for serving
- 1 garlic clove, minced
- 6 ounces tortilla chips
- ½ cup refried beans
- 8 ounces cheddar cheese, shredded (2 cups)
- 2 scallions, sliced thin
- 1 jalapeño chile, stemmed, seeded, and sliced thin
- ¼ cup sour cream

Directions:

1. Combine tomatoes, onion, lime juice, and garlic in bowl and season with salt and pepper to taste; set salsa aside until ready to serve.

2. Adjust toaster oven rack to lowest position and preheat the toaster oven to 400 degrees. Spread half of chips in even layer in 8-inch square baking dish or pan. Dollop ¼ cup refried beans in 1 tablespoon-size portions over chips, then sprinkle evenly with 1 cup cheddar. Repeat with remaining chips, ¼ cup refried beans, and 1 cup cheddar.

3. Bake nachos until cheese is melted, 7 to 12 minutes. Remove nachos from toaster oven, let cool for 2 minutes, then sprinkle with scallions and jalapeño. Along edge of nachos, drop scoops of salsa and sour cream. Serve immediately with lime wedges.

Sweet Or Savory Baked Sweet Potatoes

Servings: 6

Cooking Time: 60 Minutes

Ingredients:

- 6 medium sweet potatoes, scrubbed
- Cinnamon Butter
- Salted Garlic Herb Butter

Directions:

1. Preheat the toaster oven to 450ºF. Line a 15x10-inch baking pan with foil.
2. Prick each sweet potato several times with a fork and place on baking pan.
3. Bake 45 to 1 hour or until fork tender. Serve with Cinnamon Butter or Salted Garlic Herb Butter.

Panko-breaded Onion Rings

Servings: 4

Cooking Time: 12 Minutes

Ingredients:

- 1 large sweet onion, cut into ½-inch slices and rings separated
- 2 cups ice water
- ½ cup all-purpose flour
- 1 teaspoon paprika
- 1 teaspoon salt
- ½ teaspoon black pepper
- ½ teaspoon garlic powder
- ¼ teaspoon onion powder
- 1 egg, whisked
- 2 tablespoons milk
- 1 cup breadcrumbs

Directions:

1. Preheat the toaster oven to 400°F.
2. In a large bowl, soak the onion rings in the water for 5 minutes. Drain and pat dry with a towel.
3. In a medium bowl, place the flour, paprika, salt, pepper, garlic powder, and onion powder.
4. In a second bowl, whisk together the egg and milk.
5. In a third bowl, place the breadcrumbs.
6. To bread the onion rings, dip them first into the flour mixture, then into the egg mixture (shaking off the excess), and then into the breadcrumbs. Place the coated onion rings onto a plate while you bread all the rings.
7. Place the onion rings into the air fryer oven in a single layer, sometimes nesting smaller rings into larger rings. Spray with cooking spray. Air-fry for 3 minutes, turn the rings over, and spray with more cooking spray. Air-fry for another 3 to 5 minutes. Cook the rings in batches; you may need to do 2 or 3 batches, depending on the size of your air fryer oven.

Arancini With Sun-dried Tomatoes And Mozzarella

Servings: 6

Cooking Time: 15 Minutes

Ingredients:

- 1 tablespoon olive oil
- ½ small onion, finely chopped
- 1 cup Arborio rice
- ¼ cup white wine or dry vermouth
- 1 cup vegetable or chicken stock
- 1½ cups water
- 1 teaspoon salt
- freshly ground black pepper
- ⅓ cup grated Parmigiano-Reggiano cheese
- 2 to 3 ounces mozzarella cheese
- 2 eggs, lightly beaten
- ¼ cup chopped oil-packed sun-dried tomatoes
- 1½ cups Italian seasoned breadcrumbs, divided
- olive oil
- marinara sauce, for serving

Directions:

1. .Start by cooking the Arborio rice.
2. Stovetop Method: Preheat a medium saucepan over medium heat. Add the olive oil and sauté the onion until it starts to become tender – about 5 minutes. Add the rice and stir well to coat all the grains of rice. Add the white wine or vermouth. Let this simmer and get absorbed by the rice. Then add the stock and water, cover, reduce the heat to low and simmer for 20 minutes.
3. Pressure-Cooker Method: Preheat the pressure cooker using the BROWN setting. Add the oil and cook the onion for a few minutes. Add the rice, wine, stock, water, salt and freshly ground black pepper, give everything one good stir and lock the lid in place. Pressure cook on HIGH for 7 minutes. Reduce the pressure with the QUICK-RELEASE method and carefully remove the lid.
4. Taste the rice to make sure it is tender. Season with salt and freshly ground black pepper and stir in the grated Parmigiano-Reggiano cheese. Spread the rice out onto a baking sheet to cool.
5. While the rice is cooling, cut the mozzarella into ¾-inch cubes.
6. Once the rice has cooled, combine the rice with the eggs, sun-dried tomatoes and ½ cup of the breadcrumbs. Place the remaining breadcrumbs in a shallow dish. Shape the rice mixture into 12 balls. Press a hole in the rice ball with your finger and push one or two cubes of mozzarella cheese into the hole. Mold the rice back into a ball, enclosing the cheese. Roll the finished rice balls in the breadcrumbs and place them on a baking sheet while you make the remaining rice balls. Spray or brush the rice balls with olive oil.
7. Preheat the toaster oven to 380°F.
8. Cook 6 arancini at a time. Air-fry for 10 minutes. Gently turn the arancini over, brush or spray with oil again and air-fry for another 5 minutes. Serve warm with the marinara sauce.

Breaded Zucchini

Servings: 4

Cooking Time: 10 Minutes

Ingredients:

- 1 cup all-purpose flour
- 2 large eggs
- 1½ cups panko bread crumbs
- ½ cup grated Parmesan cheese
- Sea salt, for seasoning
- Freshly ground black pepper, for seasoning
- Oil spray (hand-pumped)
- 2 zucchini, cut into ¼-inch slices

Directions:

1. Preheat the toaster oven on AIR FRY to 350°F for 5 minutes.

2. Sprinkle the flour onto a plate.

3. In a small bowl, beat the eggs and place the bowl next to the flour.

4. In a medium bowl, stir the bread crumbs and cheese and season the mixture with salt and pepper. Place the bowl next to the eggs.

5. Place the air-fryer basket on the baking sheet and generously spray the rack with oil.

6. Dredge a zucchini slice in the flour, then the eggs, then the bread crumb mixture until well coated. Place the slice in the basket and repeat with the remaining zucchini slices. Spray the slices on both sides with oil.

7. In position 2, air fry for 10 minutes, turning once at 5 minutes, until golden brown and crispy. Serve immediately.

Pizza Bagel Bites

Servings: 2

Cooking Time: 5 Minutes

Ingredients:

- 2 Mini bagel(s), split into two rings
- ¼ cup Purchased pizza sauce
- ½ cup Finely grated or shredded cheese, such as Parmesan cheese, semi-firm mozzarella, fontina, or (preferably) a cheese blend

Directions:

1. Preheat the toaster oven to 375°F .

2. Spread the cut side of each bagel half with 1 tablespoon pizza sauce; top each half with 2 tablespoons shredded cheese.

3. When the machine is at temperature, put the bagels cheese side up in the air fryer oven in one layer. Air-fry undisturbed for 4 minutes, or until the cheese has melted and is gooey. You may need to air-fry the pizza bagel bites for 1 minute extra if the temperature is at 360°F.

4. Use a nonstick-safe spatula to transfer the topped bagel halves to a wire rack. Cool for at least 5 minutes before serving.

Foolproof Baked White Rice

Servings: 2

Cooking Time: 45 Minutes

Ingredients:

- 1¾ cups boiling water
- 1 cup long-grain white rice, rinsed
- 1 teaspoon extra-virgin olive oil
- ¼ teaspoon table salt

Directions:

1. Adjust toaster oven rack to middle position and preheat the toaster oven to 450 degrees. Combine all ingredients in 8-inch square baking dish or pan. Cover dish tightly with aluminum foil and bake until liquid is absorbed and rice is tender, 20 to 30 minutes, rotating dish halfway through baking.
2. Remove dish from oven, uncover, and fluff rice with fork, scraping up any rice that has stuck to bottom. Re-cover dish with foil and let rice sit for 10 minutes. Season with salt and pepper to taste. Serve.

Sesame Green Beans

Servings: 4

Cooking Time: 8 Minutes

Ingredients:

- 1 pound green beans, stems trimmed
- 1 tablespoon olive oil
- 1 teaspoon sesame oil
- 1 tablespoon sesame seeds
- Pinch sea salt

Directions:

1. Preheat the toaster oven to 350°F on AIR FRY for 5 minutes.
2. In a large bowl, toss the green beans, olive oil, and sesame oil.
3. Place the air-fryer basket in the baking tray and spread the beans in the basket.
4. Place the tray in position 2 and air fry for 8 minutes, shaking the basket at the halfway point. The beans should be lightly golden and fragrant.
5. Transfer the beans to a serving plate and serve topped with the sesame seeds and seasoned with salt.

Barbecue Chicken Nachos

Servings: 3
Cooking Time: 5 Minutes

Ingredients:

- 3 heaping cups (a little more than 3 ounces) Corn tortilla chips (gluten-free, if a concern)
- ¾ cup Shredded deboned and skinned rotisserie chicken meat (gluten-free, if a concern)
- 3 tablespoons Canned black beans, drained and rinsed
- 9 rings Pickled jalapeño slices
- 4 Small pickled cocktail onions, halved
- 3 tablespoons Barbecue sauce (any sort)
- ¾ cup (about 3 ounces) Shredded Cheddar cheese

Directions:

1. Preheat the toaster oven to 400°F.
2. Cut a circle of parchment paper to line a 6-inch round cake pan for a small air fryer oven, a 7-inch round cake pan for a medium air fryer oven, or an 8-inch round cake pan for a large machine.
3. Fill the pan with an even layer of about two-thirds of the chips. Sprinkle the chicken evenly over the chips. Set the pan in the air fryer oven and air-fry undisturbed for 2 minutes.
4. Remove the pan from the machine. Scatter the beans, jalapeño rings, and pickled onion halves over the chicken. Drizzle the barbecue sauce over everything, then sprinkle the cheese on top.
5. Return the pan to the machine and air-fry undisturbed for 3 minutes, or until the cheese has melted and is bubbly. Remove the pan from the machine and cool for a couple of minutes before serving.

Bacon Corn Muffins

Servings: 6
Cooking Time: 17 Minutes

Ingredients:

- 1 1/4 cups self rising cornmeal mix
- 3/4 cup buttermilk
- 1/3 cup chopped cooked bacon
- 1/4 cup butter, melted
- 1 large egg, slightly beaten

Directions:

1. Preheat toaster oven to 425°F on CONVECTION setting.
2. Stir cornmeal mix, buttermilk, bacon, butter and egg until blended.
3. Spoon batter into lightly greased muffin pan, filling 3/4 full.
4. Bake 15 to 17 minutes until toothpick inserted in center comes out clean.
5. Cool 10 minutes on wire rack; remove.

Spicy Pigs In A Blanket

Servings: 20

Cooking Time: 15 Minutes

Ingredients:
- 6 tablespoons unsalted butter, melted
- 1 teaspoon poppy seeds
- 1 teaspoon dry minced onion
- ½ teaspoon granulated garlic
- ½ teaspoon dry mustard
- ¼ teaspoon red pepper flakes
- 1 (8-ounce) tube refrigerated crescent dough sheets
- 1 (12-ounce) package cocktail smoked sausages

Directions:
1. Combine the butter, poppy seeds, onion, garlic, dry mustard, and red pepper flakes in a small bowl.
2. Lightly flour a clean surface and unroll the crescent roll sheet. Cut the sheet in half down the center, then cut those pieces in half the other way. Continue to make vertical and horizontal cuts until you have 32 strips of dough.
3. Preheat the toaster oven to 375°F.
4. Drain and pat dry the cocktail sausages using paper towels. Wrap each sausage in a strip of dough. Place about half on a 12 x 12-inch baking pan, seam side down.
5. Stir the butter mixture again to distribute all the spices and brush generously over the pastry-wrapped sausages. Bake for 14 to 15 minutes, or until they are golden brown. Repeat with the remaining half of the ingredients. Allow to cool slightly before serving.

FISH AND SEAFOOD

Beer-battered Cod

Servings: 3
Cooking Time: 12 Minutes

Ingredients:

- 1½ cups All-purpose flour
- 3 tablespoons Old Bay seasoning
- 1 Large egg(s)
- ¼ cup Amber beer, pale ale, or IPA
- 3 4-ounce skinless cod fillets
- Vegetable oil spray

Directions:

1. Preheat the toaster oven to 400°F.
2. Set up and fill two shallow soup plates or small pie plates on your counter: one with the flour, whisked with the Old Bay until well combined; and one with the egg(s), whisked with the beer until foamy and uniform.
3. Dip a piece of cod in the flour mixture, turning it to coat on all sides (not just the top and bottom). Gently shake off any excess flour and dip the fish in the egg mixture, turning it to coat. Let any excess egg mixture slip back into the rest, then set the fish back in the flour mixture and coat it again, then back in the egg mixture for a second wash, then back in the flour mixture for a third time. Coat the fish on all sides with vegetable oil spray and set it aside. "Batter" the remaining piece(s) of cod in the same way.
4. Set the coated cod fillets in the air fryer oven with as much space between them as possible. They should not touch. Air-fry undisturbed for 12 minutes, or until brown and crisp.
5. Use kitchen tongs to gently transfer the fish to a wire rack. Cool for only a couple of minutes before serving.

Stuffed Shrimp

Servings: 4

Cooking Time: 12 Minutes

Ingredients:

- 16 tail-on shrimp, peeled and deveined (last tail section intact)
- ¾ cup crushed panko breadcrumbs
- oil for misting or cooking spray
- Stuffing
- 2 6-ounce cans lump crabmeat
- 2 tablespoons chopped shallots
- 2 tablespoons chopped green onions
- 2 tablespoons chopped celery
- 2 tablespoons chopped green bell pepper
- ½ cup crushed saltine crackers
- 1 teaspoon Old Bay Seasoning
- 1 teaspoon garlic powder
- ¼ teaspoon ground thyme
- 2 teaspoons dried parsley flakes
- 2 teaspoons fresh lemon juice
- 2 teaspoons Worcestershire sauce
- 1 egg, beaten

Directions:

1. Rinse shrimp. Remove tail section (shell) from 4 shrimp, discard, and chop the meat finely.
2. To prepare the remaining 12 shrimp, cut a deep slit down the back side so that the meat lies open flat. Do not cut all the way through.
3. Preheat the toaster oven to 360°F.
4. Place chopped shrimp in a large bowl with all of the stuffing ingredients and stir to combine.
5. Divide stuffing into 12 portions, about 2 tablespoons each.
6. Place one stuffing portion onto the back of each shrimp and form into a ball or oblong shape. Press firmly so that stuffing sticks together and adheres to shrimp.
7. Gently roll each stuffed shrimp in panko crumbs and mist with oil or cooking spray.
8. Place 6 shrimp in air fryer oven and air-fry at 360°F for 10 minutes. Mist with oil or spray and cook 2 minutes longer or until stuffing cooks through inside and is crispy outside.
9. Repeat step 8 to cook remaining shrimp.

Garlic And Dill Salmon

Servings: 2

Cooking Time: 8 Minutes

Ingredients:

- 12 ounces salmon filets with skin
- 2 tablespoons melted butter
- 1 tablespoon extra-virgin olive oil
- 2 garlic cloves, minced
- 1 tablespoon fresh dill
- ½ teaspoon sea salt
- ½ lemon

Directions:

1. Pat the salmon dry with paper towels.
2. In a small bowl, mix together the melted butter, olive oil, garlic, and dill.
3. Sprinkle the top of the salmon with sea salt. Brush all sides of the salmon with the garlic and dill butter.
4. Preheat the toaster oven to 350°F.
5. Place the salmon, skin side down, in the air fryer oven. Air-fry for 6 to 8 minutes, or until the fish flakes in the center.
6. Remove the salmon and plate on a serving platter. Squeeze fresh lemon over the top of the salmon. Serve immediately.

Pecan-topped Sole

Servings: 4

Cooking Time: 12 Minutes

Ingredients:

- 4 (4-ounce) sole fillets
- Sea salt, for seasoning
- Freshly ground black pepper, for seasoning
- 1 cup crushed pecans
- ½ cup seasoned bread crumbs
- 1 large egg
- 2 tablespoons water
- Oil spray (hand-pumped)

Directions:

1. Preheat the toaster oven to 375°F on BAKE for 5 minutes.
2. Line the baking tray with parchment paper.
3. Pat the fish dry with paper towels and lightly season with salt and pepper.
4. In a small bowl, stir the pecans and bread crumbs.
5. In another small bowl, beat the egg and water until well blended.
6. Dredge the fish in the egg mixture, shaking off any excess, then in the nut mixture.
7. Place the fish in the baking sheet and repeat with the remaining fish.
8. Lightly spray the fillets with the oil on both sides.
9. In position 2, bake until golden and crispy, turning halfway, for 12 minutes in total. Serve.

Ginger Miso Calamari

Servings: 4
Cooking Time: 10 Minutes

Ingredients:

- 15 ounces calamari, cleaned
- Sauce:
- 2 tablespoons dry white wine
- 2 tablespoons white miso
- 1 tablespoon balsamic vinegar
- 1 teaspoon honey
- 1 teaspoon toasted sesame oil
- 1 teaspoon olive oil
- 1 tablespoon grated fresh ginger
- Salt and white pepper to taste

Directions:

1. Slice the calamari bodies into ½-inch rings, leaving the tentacles uncut. Set aside.
2. Whisk together the sauce ingredients in a bowl. Transfer the mixture to a baking pan and add the calamari, mixing well to coat.
3. BROIL for 20 minutes, turning with tongs every 5 minutes, or until cooked but not rubbery. Serve with the sauce.

Scallops In Orange Sauce

Servings: 4
Cooking Time: 3 Minutes

Ingredients:

- Broiling mixture:
- 1 cup orange juice
- 1 teaspoon soy sauce
- 2 garlic cloves, finely minced
- 1 teaspoon grated orange zest
- 1½ pounds (3 cups) bay scallops, rinsed and drained
- 1 7-ounce can sliced water chestnuts, drained well
- 2 tablespoons chopped watercress

Directions:

1. Whisk together the broiling mixture ingredients in a small bowl and transfer to an 8½ × 8½ × 2-inch oiled or nonstick square (cake) pan.
2. BROIL the sauce for 10 minutes to reduce the liquid and meld the flavors. Remove the pan from the oven and add the scallops, spooning the sauce over them.
3. BROIL for 3 minutes, or until opaque. Serve the scallops with the sauce and garnish with the sliced water chestnuts and chopped watercress.

Sweet Chili Shrimp

Servings: 4

Cooking Time: 6 Minutes

Ingredients:

- 1 pound jumbo shrimp, peeled and deveined
- ¼ cup sweet chili sauce
- 1 lime, zested and juiced
- 1 tablespoon soy sauce
- 1 tablespoon honey
- 1 tablespoon olive oil
- 1 large garlic clove, minced
- ½ teaspoon salt
- ¼ teaspoon pepper
- 1 green onion, thinly sliced, for garnish

Directions:

1. Place the shrimp in a large bowl. Whisk all the remaining ingredients except the green onion in a separate bowl.
2. Pour sauce over the shrimp and toss to coat.
3. Preheat the toaster Oven to 430°F.
4. Line the food tray with foil, place shrimp on the tray, then insert at top position in the preheated oven.
5. Select the Air Fry function, adjust time to 6 minutes, and press Start/Pause.
6. Remove shrimp and garnish with sliced green onions.

Fish Tacos With Jalapeño-lime Sauce

Servings: 4

Cooking Time: 7 Minutes

Ingredients:

- Fish Tacos
- 1 pound fish fillets
- ¼ teaspoon cumin
- ¼ teaspoon coriander
- ⅛ teaspoon ground red pepper
- 1 tablespoon lime zest
- ¼ teaspoon smoked paprika
- 1 teaspoon oil
- cooking spray
- 6–8 corn or flour tortillas (6-inch size)

- Jalapeño-Lime Sauce
- ½ cup sour cream
- 1 tablespoon lime juice
- ¼ teaspoon grated lime zest
- ½ teaspoon minced jalapeño (flesh only)
- ¼ teaspoon cumin
- Napa Cabbage Garnish
- 1 cup shredded Napa cabbage
- ¼ cup slivered red or green bell pepper
- ¼ cup slivered onion

Directions:

1. Slice the fish fillets into strips approximately ½-inch thick.

2. Put the strips into a sealable plastic bag along with the cumin, coriander, red pepper, lime zest, smoked paprika, and oil. Massage seasonings into the fish until evenly distributed.

3. Spray air fryer oven with nonstick cooking spray and place seasoned fish inside.

4. Air-fry at 390°F for approximately 5 minutes. Distribute fish. Cook an additional 2 minutes, until fish flakes easily.

5. While the fish is cooking, prepare the Jalapeño-Lime Sauce by mixing the sour cream, lime juice, lime zest, jalapeño, and cumin together to make a smooth sauce. Set aside.

6. Mix the cabbage, bell pepper, and onion together and set aside.

7. To warm refrigerated tortillas, wrap in damp paper towels and microwave for 30 to 60 seconds.

8. To serve, spoon some of fish into a warm tortilla. Add one or two tablespoons Napa Cabbage Garnish and drizzle with Jalapeño-Lime Sauce.

Baked Tomato Pesto Bluefish

Servings: 2

Cooking Time: 23 Minutes

Ingredients:

- 2 plum tomatoes
- 2 tablespoons tomato paste
- ¼ cup fresh basil leaves
- 1 tablespoon olive oil
- 2 garlic cloves
- 2 tablespoons pine nuts
- ¼ cup grated Parmesan cheese
- 1 teaspoon dried oregano
- Salt to taste
- 2 6-ounce bluefish fillets

Directions:

1. Preheat the toaster oven to 400° F.
2. Process the pesto ingredients in a blender or food processor until smooth.
3. Place the bluefish fillets in an oiled or nonstick 8½ × 8½ × 2-inch square baking (cake) pan.
4. BAKE, covered, for 15 minutes, or until the fish flakes with a fork. Remove from the oven, uncover, and spread the pesto mixture on both sides of the fillets.
5. BROIL, uncovered, for 8 minutes, or until the pesto is lightly browned.

Romaine Wraps With Shrimp Filling

Servings: 4

Cooking Time: 8 Minutes

Ingredients:

- Filling:
- 1 6-ounce can tiny shrimp, drained, or 1 cup fresh shrimp, peeled, cooked, and chopped
- ¾ cup canned chickpeas, mashed into 1 tablespoon olive oil
- 2 tablespoons chopped fresh parsley
- 2 tablespoons grated carrot
- 2 tablespoons chopped bell pepper
- 2 tablespoons minced onion
- 2 tablespoons lemon juice
- 1 teaspoon soy sauce
- Freshly ground black pepper to taste
- 4 large romaine lettuce leaves Olive oil
- 3 tablespoons lemon juice
- 1 teaspoon paprika

Directions:

1. Combine the filling ingredients in a bowl, adjusting the seasonings to taste. Spoon equal portions of the filling into the centers of the romaine leaves. Fold the leaves in half, pressing the filling together, overlap the leaf edges, and skewer with toothpicks to fasten. Carefully place the leaves in an oiled or nonstick 8½ × 8½ × 2-inch square baking (cake) pan. Lightly spray or brush the lettuce rolls with olive oil.
2. BROIL for 8 minutes, or until the filling is cooked and the leaves are lightly browned. Remove from the oven, remove the toothpicks, band drizzle with the lemon juice and sprinkle with paprika.

Crab Cakes

Servings: 4
Cooking Time: 9 Minutes

Ingredients:

- 1 pound lump crab meat, checked for shells
- ⅓ cup breadcrumbs
- ¼ cup finely chopped onions
- ¼ cup finely chopped red bell peppers
- ¼ cup finely chopped parsley
- ¼ teaspoon sea salt
- 2 eggs, whisked
- ¾ cup mayonnaise, divided
- ¼ cup sour cream
- 1 lemon, divided
- ¼ cup sweet pickle relish
- 1 tablespoon prepared mustard

Directions:

1. In a large bowl, mix together the crab meat, breadcrumbs, onions, bell peppers, parsley, sea salt, eggs, and ¼ cup of the mayonnaise.

2. Preheat the toaster oven to 380°F.

3. Form 8 patties with the crab cake mixture. Line the air fryer oven with parchment paper and place the crab cakes on the parchment paper. Spray with cooking spray. Air-fry for 4 minutes, turn over the crab cakes, spray with cooking spray, and air-fry for an additional 3 to 5 minutes, or until golden brown and the edges are crispy. Cook in batches as needed.

4. Meanwhile, make the sauce. In a small bowl, mix together the remaining ½ cup of mayonnaise, the sour cream, the juice from ½ of the lemon, the pickle relish, and the mustard.

5. Place the cooked crab cakes on a serving platter and serve with the remaining ½ lemon cut into wedges and the dipping sauce.

Beer-breaded Halibut Fish Tacos

Servings: 4

Cooking Time: 10 Minutes

Ingredients:
- 1 pound halibut, cut into 1-inch strips
- 1 cup light beer
- 1 jalapeño, minced and divided
- 1 clove garlic, minced
- ¼ teaspoon ground cumin
- ½ cup cornmeal
- ¼ cup all-purpose flour
- 1¼ teaspoons sea salt, divided
- 2 cups shredded cabbage
- 1 lime, juiced and divided
- ¼ cup Greek yogurt
- ¼ cup mayonnaise
- 1 cup grape tomatoes, quartered
- ½ cup chopped cilantro
- ¼ cup chopped onion
- 1 egg, whisked
- 8 corn tortillas

Directions:
1. In a shallow baking dish, place the fish, the beer, 1 teaspoon of the minced jalapeño, the garlic, and the cumin. Cover and refrigerate for 30 minutes.
2. Meanwhile, in a medium bowl, mix together the cornmeal, flour, and ½ teaspoon of the salt.
3. In large bowl, mix together the shredded cabbage, 1 tablespoon of the lime juice, the Greek yogurt, the mayonnaise, and ½ teaspoon of the salt.
4. In a small bowl, make the pico de gallo by mixing together the tomatoes, cilantro, onion, ¼ teaspoon of the salt, the remaining jalapeño, and the remaining lime juice.
5. Remove the fish from the refrigerator and discard the marinade. Dredge the fish in the whisked egg; then dredge the fish in the cornmeal flour mixture, until all pieces of fish have been breaded.
6. Preheat the toaster oven to 350°F.
7. Place the fish in the air fryer oven and spray liberally with cooking spray. Air-fry for 6 minutes, flip the fish, and cook another 4 minutes.
8. While the fish is cooking, heat the tortillas in a heavy skillet for 1 to 2 minutes over high heat.
9. To assemble the tacos, place the battered fish on the heated tortillas, and top with slaw and pico de gallo. Serve immediately.

Cajun Flounder Fillets

Servings: 2

Cooking Time: 5 Minutes

Ingredients:

- 2 4-ounce skinless flounder fillet(s)
- 2 teaspoons Peanut oil
- 1 teaspoon Purchased or homemade Cajun dried seasoning blend

Directions:

1. Preheat the toaster oven to 400°F.

2. Oil the fillet(s) by drizzling on the peanut oil, then gently rubbing in the oil with your clean, dry fingers. Sprinkle the seasoning blend evenly over both sides of the fillet(s).

3. When the machine is at temperature, set the fillet(s) in the air fryer oven. If working with more than one fillet, they should not touch, although they may be quite close together, depending on the air fryer oven's size. Air-fry undisturbed for 5 minutes, or until lightly browned and cooked through.

4. Use a nonstick-safe spatula to transfer the fillets to a serving platter or plate(s). Serve at once.

Crispy Smelts

Servings: 3

Cooking Time: 20 Minutes

Ingredients:

- 1 pound Cleaned smelts
- 3 tablespoons Tapioca flour
- Vegetable oil spray
- To taste Coarse sea salt or kosher salt

Directions:

1. Preheat the toaster oven to 400°F.

2. Toss the smelts and tapioca flour in a large bowl until the little fish are evenly coated.

3. Lay the smelts out on a large cutting board. Lightly coat both sides of each fish with vegetable oil spray.

4. When the machine is at temperature, set the smelts close together in the air fryer oven, with a few even overlapping on top. Air-fry undisturbed for 20 minutes, until lightly browned and crisp.

5. Remove from the machine and turn out the fish onto a wire rack. The smelts will most likely come out as one large block, or maybe in a couple of large pieces. Cool for a minute or two, then sprinkle the smelts with salt and break the block(s) into much smaller sections or individual fish to serve.

Coconut-crusted Shrimp

Servings: 4
Cooking Time: 20 Minutes

Ingredients:

- Oil spray (hand-pumped)
- ½ cup all-purpose flour
- 2 large eggs
- ¾ cup unsweetened, shredded coconut
- ½ cup panko bread crumbs
- ¼ teaspoon sea salt
- 1 pound (26 to 30 count) raw extra-large shrimp, peeled and deveined with tails attached

Directions:

1. Preheat the toaster oven to 400°F on AIR FRY for 5 minutes.
2. Place the air-fryer basket in the baking tray and spray it generously with the oil.
3. Place the flour on a plate and set it on your work surface.
4. In a small bowl, whisk the eggs until well beaten and place next to the flour.
5. In a medium bowl, stir the coconut, bread crumbs, and salt, and place next to the eggs.
6. Pat the shrimp dry with paper towels. Working in two batches, dredge the shrimp in the flour, then egg, then coconut mixture, and place them in the basket. Do not crowd the basket.
7. Lightly spray the shrimp with the oil on both sides and in position 2, air fry for 10 minutes, turning halfway through, until golden brown.
8. Repeat with the remaining shrimp, covering the cooked shrimp loosely with foil to keep them warm. Serve.

Oven-crisped Fish Fillets With Salsa

Servings: 4
Cooking Time: 14 Minutes

Ingredients:

- Coating ingredients:
- 1 cup cornmeal
- 1 teaspoon garlic powder
- 1 teaspoon ground cumin
- 1 teaspoon paprika
- Salt to taste
- 4 6-ounce fish fillets, approximately
- ¼ to ½ inch thick
- 2 tablespoons vegetable oil

Directions:

1. Combine the coating ingredients in a small bowl, blending well. Transfer to a large plate, spreading evenly over the surface. Brush the fillets with vegetable oil and press both sides of each fillet into the coating.
2. BROIL an oiled or nonstick 8½ × 8½ × 2-inch square baking (cake) pan for 1 or 2 minutes to preheat. Remove the pan and place the fillets in the hot pan, laying them flat.
3. BROIL for 7 minutes, then remove the pan from the oven and carefully turn the fillets with a spatula. Broil for another 7 minutes, or until the fish flakes easily with a fork and the coating is crisped to your preference. Serve immediately.

Shrimp With Jalapeño Dip

Servings: 4

Cooking Time: 10 Minutes

Ingredients:

- Seasonings:
- 1 teaspoon ground cumin
- 1 tablespoon minced garlic
- 1 teaspoon paprika
- 1 teaspoon chili powder
- Pinch of cayenne
- Salt to taste
- 1½ pounds large shrimp, peeled and deveined

Directions:

1. Combine the seasonings in a plastic bag, add the shrimp, and shake well to coat. Transfer the shrimp to an oiled or nonstick 8½ × 8½ × 2-inch square baking (cake) pan.

2. BROIL for 5 minutes. Remove the pan from the oven and turn the shrimp with tongs. Broil 5 minutes again, or until the shrimp are cooked (they should be firm but not rubbery.) Serve with Jalapeño Dip.

Shrimp Patties

Servings: 4

Cooking Time: 10 Minutes

Ingredients:

- ½ pound shelled and deveined raw shrimp
- ¼ cup chopped red bell pepper
- ¼ cup chopped green onion
- ¼ cup chopped celery
- 2 cups cooked sushi rice
- ½ teaspoon garlic powder
- ½ teaspoon Old Bay Seasoning
- ½ teaspoon salt
- 2 teaspoons Worcestershire sauce
- ½ cup plain breadcrumbs
- oil for misting or cooking spray

Directions:

1. Finely chop the shrimp. You can do this in a food processor, but it takes only a few pulses. Be careful not to overprocess into mush.

2. Place shrimp in a large bowl and add all other ingredients except the breadcrumbs and oil. Stir until well combined.

3. Preheat the toaster oven to 390°F.

4. Shape shrimp mixture into 8 patties, no more than ½-inch thick. Roll patties in breadcrumbs and mist with oil or cooking spray.

5. Place 4 shrimp patties in air fryer oven and air-fry at 390°F for 10 minutes, until shrimp cooks through and outside is crispy.

6. Repeat step 5 to cook remaining shrimp patties.

Pecan-crusted Tilapia

Servings: 4

Cooking Time: 8 Minutes

Ingredients:

- 1 pound skinless, boneless tilapia filets
- ¼ cup butter, melted
- 1 teaspoon minced fresh or dried rosemary
- 1 cup finely chopped pecans
- 1 teaspoon sea salt
- ¼ teaspoon paprika
- 2 tablespoons chopped parsley
- 1 lemon, cut into wedges

Directions:

1. Pat the tilapia filets dry with paper towels.
2. Pour the melted butter over the filets and flip the filets to coat them completely.
3. In a medium bowl, mix together the rosemary, pecans, salt, and paprika.
4. Preheat the toaster oven to 350°F.
5. Place the tilapia filets into the air fryer oven and top with the pecan coating. Air-fry for 6 to 8 minutes. The fish should be firm to the touch and flake easily when fully cooked.
6. Remove the fish from the air fryer oven. Top the fish with chopped parsley and serve with lemon wedges.

BEEF PORK AND LAMB

Minted Lamb Chops

Servings: 4

Cooking Time: 15 Minutes

Ingredients:

- Mint mixture:
- 4 tablespoons finely chopped fresh mint
- 2 tablespoons nonfat yogurt
- 1 tablespoon olive oil
- Salt and freshly ground black pepper to taste
- 4 lean lamb chops, fat trimmed, approximately ¾ inch thick
- 1 tablespoon balsamic vinegar

Directions:

1. Combine the mint mixture ingredients in a small bowl, stirring well to blend. Set aside. Place the lamp chops on a broiling rack with a pan underneath.

2. BROIL the lamb chops for 10 minutes, or until they are slightly pink. Remove from the oven and brush one side liberally with balsamic vinegar. Turn the chops over with tongs and spread with the mint mixture, using all of the mixture.

3. BROIL again for 5 minutes, or until lightly browned.

Orange Glazed Pork Tenderloin

Servings: 3

Cooking Time: 23 Minutes

Ingredients:

- 2 tablespoons brown sugar
- 2 teaspoons cornstarch
- 2 teaspoons Dijon mustard
- ½ cup orange juice
- ½ teaspoon soy sauce
- 2 teaspoons grated fresh ginger
- ¼ cup white wine
- zest of 1 orange
- 1 pound pork tenderloin
- salt and freshly ground black pepper
- oranges, halved (for garnish)
- fresh parsley or other green herb (for garnish)

Directions:

1. Combine the brown sugar, cornstarch, Dijon mustard, orange juice, soy sauce, ginger, white wine and orange zest in a small saucepan and bring the mixture to a boil on the stovetop. Lower the heat and simmer while you cook the pork tenderloin or until the sauce has thickened.

2. Preheat the toaster oven to 370°F.

3. Season all sides of the pork tenderloin with salt and freshly ground black pepper. Transfer the tenderloin to the air fryer oven, bending the pork into a wide "U" shape if necessary to fit in the air fryer oven. Air-fry at 370°F for 20 to 23 minutes, or until the internal temperature reaches 145°F. Flip the tenderloin over halfway through the cooking process and baste with the sauce.

4. Transfer the tenderloin to a cutting board and let it rest for 5 minutes. Slice the pork at a slight angle and serve immediately with orange halves and fresh herbs to dress it up. Drizzle any remaining glaze over the top.

Calf's Liver

Servings: 4

Cooking Time: 5 Minutes

Ingredients:

- 1 pound sliced calf's liver
- salt and pepper
- 2 eggs
- 2 tablespoons milk
- ½ cup whole wheat flour
- 1½ cups panko breadcrumbs
- ½ cup plain breadcrumbs
- ½ teaspoon salt
- ¼ teaspoon pepper
- oil for misting or cooking spray

Directions:

1. Cut liver slices crosswise into strips about ½-inch wide. Sprinkle with salt and pepper to taste.
2. Beat together egg and milk in a shallow dish.
3. Place wheat flour in a second shallow dish.
4. In a third shallow dish, mix together panko, plain breadcrumbs, ½ teaspoon salt, and ¼ teaspoon pepper.
5. Preheat the toaster oven to 390°F.
6. Dip liver strips in flour, egg wash, and then breadcrumbs, pressing in coating slightly to make crumbs stick.
7. Cooking half the liver at a time, place strips in air fryer oven in a single layer, close but not touching. Air-fry at 390°F for 5 minutes or until done to your preference.
8. Repeat step 7 to cook remaining liver.

Albóndigas

Servings: 4

Cooking Time: 15 Minutes

Ingredients:

- 1 pound Lean ground pork
- 3 tablespoons Very finely chopped trimmed scallions
- 3 tablespoons Finely chopped fresh cilantro leaves
- 3 tablespoons Plain panko bread crumbs (gluten-free, if a concern)
- 3 tablespoons Dry white wine, dry sherry, or unsweetened apple juice
- 1½ teaspoons Minced garlic
- 1¼ teaspoons Mild smoked paprika
- ¾ teaspoon Dried oregano
- ¾ teaspoon Table salt
- ¼ teaspoon Ground black pepper
- Olive oil spray

Directions:

1. Preheat the toaster oven to 400°F.

2. Mix the ground pork, scallions, cilantro, bread crumbs, wine or its substitute, garlic, smoked paprika, oregano, salt, and pepper in a bowl until the herbs and spices are evenly distributed in the mixture.

3. Lightly coat your clean hands with olive oil spray, then form the ground pork mixture into balls, using 2 tablespoons for each one. Spray your hands frequently so that the meat mixture doesn't stick.

4. Set the balls in the air fryer oven so that they're not touching, even if they're close together. Air-fry undisturbed for 15 minutes, or until well browned and an instant-read meat thermometer inserted into one or two balls registers 165°F.

5. Use a nonstick-safe spatula and kitchen tongs for balance to gently transfer the fragile balls to a wire rack to cool for 5 minutes before serving.

Indian Fry Bread Tacos

Servings: 4

Cooking Time: 20 Minutes

Ingredients:

- 1 cup all-purpose flour
- 1½ teaspoons salt, divided
- 1½ teaspoons baking powder
- ¼ cup milk
- ¼ cup warm water
- ½ pound lean ground beef
- One 14.5-ounce can pinto beans, drained and rinsed
- 1 tablespoon taco seasoning
- ½ cup shredded cheddar cheese
- 2 cups shredded lettuce
- ¼ cup black olives, chopped
- 1 Roma tomato, diced
- 1 avocado, diced
- 1 lime

Directions:

1. In a large bowl, whisk together the flour, 1 teaspoon of the salt, and baking powder. Make a well in the center and add in the milk and water. Form a ball and gently knead the dough four times. Cover the bowl with a damp towel, and set aside.

2. Preheat the toaster oven to 380°F.

3. In a medium bowl, mix together the ground beef, beans, and taco seasoning. Crumble the meat mixture into the air fryer oven and air-fry for 5 minutes; toss the meat and cook an additional 2 to 3 minutes, or until cooked fully. Place the cooked meat in a bowl for taco assembly; season with the remaining ½ teaspoon salt as desired.

4. On a floured surface, place the dough. Cut the dough into 4 equal parts. Using a rolling pin, roll out each piece of dough to 5 inches in diameter. Spray the dough with cooking spray and place in the air fryer oven, working in batches as needed. Air-fry for 3 minutes, flip over, spray with cooking spray, and air-fry for an additional 1 to 3 minutes, until golden and puffy.

5. To assemble, place the fry breads on a serving platter. Equally divide the meat and bean mixture on top of the fry bread. Divide the cheese, lettuce, olives, tomatoes, and avocado among the four tacos. Squeeze lime over the top prior to serving.

Chicken Fried Steak

Servings: 4
Cooking Time: 15 Minutes

Ingredients:
- 2 eggs
- ½ cup buttermilk
- 1½ cups flour
- ¾ teaspoon salt
- ½ teaspoon pepper
- 1 pound beef cube steaks
- salt and pepper
- oil for misting or cooking spray

Directions:
1. Beat together eggs and buttermilk in a shallow dish.
2. In another shallow dish, stir together the flour, ½ teaspoon salt, and ¼ teaspoon pepper.
3. Season cube steaks with remaining salt and pepper to taste. Dip in flour, buttermilk egg wash, and then flour again.
4. Spray both sides of steaks with oil or cooking spray.
5. Cooking in 2 batches, place steaks in air fryer oven in single layer. Air-fry at 360°F for 10 minutes. Spray tops of steaks with oil and cook 5 minutes or until meat is well done.
6. Repeat to cook remaining steaks.

Calzones South Of The Border

Servings: 8

Cooking Time: 8 Minutes

Ingredients:

- Filling
- ¼ pound ground pork sausage
- ½ teaspoon chile powder
- ¼ teaspoon ground cumin
- ⅛ teaspoon garlic powder
- ⅛ teaspoon onion powder
- ⅛ teaspoon oregano
- ½ cup ricotta cheese
- 1 ounce sharp Cheddar cheese, shredded
- 2 ounces Pepper Jack cheese, shredded
- 1 4-ounce can chopped green chiles, drained
- oil for misting or cooking spray
- salsa, sour cream, or guacamole
- Crust
- 2 cups white wheat flour, plus more for kneading and rolling
- 1 package (¼ ounce) RapidRise yeast
- 1 teaspoon salt
- ½ teaspoon chile powder
- ½ teaspoon ground cumin
- 1 cup warm water (115°F to 125°F)
- 2 teaspoons olive oil

Directions:

1. Crumble sausage into air fryer oven baking pan and stir in the filling seasonings: chile powder, cumin, garlic powder, onion powder, and oregano. Air-fry at 390°F for 2 minutes. Stir, breaking apart, and air-fry for 3 to 4 minutes, until well done. Remove and set aside on paper towels to drain.

2. To make dough, combine flour, yeast, salt, chile powder, and cumin. Stir in warm water and oil until soft dough forms. Turn out onto lightly floured board and knead for 3 or 4 minutes. Let dough rest for 10 minutes.

3. Place the three cheeses in a medium bowl. Add cooked sausage and chiles and stir until well mixed.

4. Cut dough into 8 pieces.

5. Working with 4 pieces of the dough, press each into a circle about 5 inches in diameter. Top each dough circle with 2 heaping tablespoons of filling. Fold over into a half-moon shape and press edges together. Seal edges firmly to prevent leakage. Spray both sides with oil or cooking spray.

6. Place 4 calzones in air fryer oven and air-fry at 360°F for 5 minutes. Mist with oil or spray and air-fry for 3 minutes, until crust is done and nicely browned.

7. While the first batch is cooking, press out the remaining dough, fill, and shape into calzones.

8. Spray both sides with oil or cooking spray and air-fry for 5 minutes. If needed, mist with oil and continue cooking for 3 minutes longer. This second batch will cook a little faster than the first because your air fryer oven is already hot.

9. Serve plain or with salsa, sour cream, or guacamole.

Spicy Flank Steak With Fresh Tomato-corn Salsa

Servings: 4

Cooking Time: 20 Minutes

Ingredients:

- 2 large tomatoes, chopped
- 1 cup fresh (or canned) corn
- ½ English cucumber, chopped
- ¼ red onion, chopped
- 1 tablespoon jalapeño pepper, chopped
- 1 tablespoon fresh cilantro, chopped
- Sea salt, for seasoning
- Freshly ground black pepper, for seasoning
- 1 pound extra-lean beef flank steak, trimmed of fat
- Olive oil, for brushing
- 1 teaspoon garlic powder
- 1 teaspoon chili powder

Directions:

1. Preheat the toaster oven to 450°F on BROIL for 5 minutes.
2. In a small bowl, stir the tomato, corn, cucumber, onion, jalapeño, and cilantro, and season with salt and pepper.
3. Rub the steak all over with the oil and then season with garlic powder, chili powder, salt, and pepper.
4. Place the air-fryer basket in the baking tray and arrange the steak in the basket.
5. In position 2, broil for 20 minutes, turning halfway through, until browned and with an internal temperature of 140°F, for medium-rare.
6. Let the steak rest for 10 minutes and then cut it very thinly against the grain.
7. Serve with the salsa.

Barbeque Ribs

Servings: 4
Cooking Time: 35 Minutes

Ingredients:

- 2 pounds pork spareribs or baby back ribs, silver skin removed
- 2 tablespoons brown sugar
- 1 teaspoon chili powder
- 1 teaspoon dry mustard
- Sea salt, for seasoning
- Freshly ground black pepper, for seasoning
- Oil spray (hand-pumped)
- 1 cup barbeque sauce

Directions:

1. Preheat the toaster oven to 375°F on AIR FRY for 5 minutes.
2. Cut the ribs into 4 bone sections or to fit in the basket.
3. In a small bowl, combine the brown sugar, chili powder, and mustard, and rub it all over the ribs.
4. Season the ribs with salt and pepper.
5. Place the air-fryer basket in the baking tray and spray it generously with the oil.
6. Arrange the ribs in the basket. There can be overlap if necessary.
7. In position 2, air fry for 35 minutes, turning halfway through, until the ribs are tender, browned, and crisp.
8. Baste the ribs with the barbeque sauce and serve.

Herbed Lamb Burgers

Servings: 4
Cooking Time: 15 Minutes

Ingredients:

- 1 pound lean ground lamb
- 1 large egg
- 1 tablespoon fresh parsley, chopped
- 2 teaspoons fresh mint, chopped
- 1 teaspoon minced garlic
- ¼ teaspoon sea salt
- ⅛ teaspoon freshly ground black pepper
- Olive oil spray (hand-pumped)
- 4 whole-wheat buns
- ¼ cup store-bought tzatziki sauce
- 1 tomato, cut into slices
- 4 thin red onion slices
- ½ cup shredded lettuce

Directions:

1. Preheat the toaster oven to 350°F on CONVECTION BROIL for 5 minutes.
2. In a large bowl, mix the lamb, egg, parsley, mint, garlic, salt, and pepper. Form the mixture into 4 patties.
3. Place the air-fryer basket in the baking tray and place the burger patties in the basket. Lightly spray the patties with the oil on both sides.
4. In position 2, broil for 15 minutes, turning halfway through.
5. Serve on the buns topped with tzatziki sauce, tomato, onion, and lettuce.

Lamb Curry

Servings: 4
Cooking Time: 40 Minutes

Ingredients:

- 1 pound lean lamb for stewing, trimmed and cut into 1 × 1-inch pieces
- 1 small onion, chopped
- 3 garlic cloves, minced
- 2 plum tomatoes, chopped
- ½ cup dry white wine
- 2 tablespoons curry powder
- Salt and cayenne to taste

Directions:

1. Preheat the toaster oven to 400° F.
2. Combine all the ingredients in an 8½ × 8½ × 4-inch ovenproof baking dish. Adjust the seasonings.
3. BAKE, covered, for 40 minutes, or until the meat is tender and the onion is cooked.

Easy Tex-mex Chimichangas

Servings: 2
Cooking Time: 8 Minutes

Ingredients:

- ¼ pound Thinly sliced deli roast beef, chopped
- ½ cup (about 2 ounces) Shredded Cheddar cheese or shredded Tex-Mex cheese blend
- ¼ cup Jarred salsa verde or salsa rojo
- ½ teaspoon Ground cumin
- ½ teaspoon Dried oregano
- 2 Burrito-size (12-inch) flour tortilla(s), not corn tortillas (gluten-free, if a concern)
- ⅔ cup Canned refried beans
- Vegetable oil spray

Directions:

1. Preheat the toaster oven to 375°F .
2. Stir the roast beef, cheese, salsa, cumin, and oregano in a bowl until well mixed.
3. Lay a tortilla on a clean, dry work surface. Spread ⅓ cup of the refried beans in the center lower third of the tortilla(s), leaving an inch on either side of the spread beans.
4. For one chimichanga, spread all of the roast beef mixture on top of the beans. For two, spread half of the roast beef mixture on each tortilla.
5. At either "end" of the filling mixture, fold the sides of the tortilla up and over the filling, partially covering it. Starting with the unfolded side of the tortilla just below the filling, roll the tortilla closed. Fold and roll the second filled tortilla, as necessary.
6. Coat the exterior of the tortilla(s) with vegetable oil spray. Set the chimichanga(s) seam side down in the air fryer oven, with at least ½ inch air space between them if you're working with two. Air-fry undisturbed for 8 minutes, or until the tortilla is lightly browned and crisp.
7. Use kitchen tongs to gently transfer the chimichanga(s) to a wire rack. Cool for at last 5 minutes or up to 20 minutes before serving.

Stuffed Pork Chops

Servings: 4

Cooking Time: 12 Minutes

Ingredients:
- 4 boneless pork chops
- ½ teaspoon salt
- ½ teaspoon black pepper
- ¼ teaspoon paprika
- 1 cup frozen spinach, defrosted and squeezed dry
- 2 cloves garlic, minced
- 2 ounces cream cheese
- ¼ cup grated Parmesan cheese
- 1 tablespoon extra-virgin olive oil

Directions:
1. Pat the pork chops with a paper towel. Make a slit in the side of each pork chop to create a pouch.
2. Season the pork chops with the salt, pepper, and paprika.
3. In a small bowl, mix together the spinach, garlic, cream cheese, and Parmesan cheese.
4. Divide the mixture into fourths and stuff the pork chop pouches. Secure the pouches with toothpicks.
5. Preheat the toaster oven to 400°F.
6. Place the stuffed pork chops in the air fryer oven and spray liberally with cooking spray. Air-fry for 6 minutes, flip and coat with more cooking spray, and cook another 6 minutes. Check to make sure the meat is cooked to an internal temperature of 145°F. Cook the pork chops in batches, as needed.

Pretzel-coated Pork Tenderloin

Servings: 4

Cooking Time: 10 Minutes

Ingredients:

- 1 Large egg white(s)
- 2 teaspoons Dijon mustard (gluten-free, if a concern)
- 1½ cups (about 6 ounces) Crushed pretzel crumbs
- 1 pound (4 sections) Pork tenderloin, cut into ¼-pound (4-ounce) sections
- Vegetable oil spray

Directions:

1. Preheat the toaster oven to 350°F .

2. Set up and fill two shallow soup plates or small pie plates on your counter: one for the egg white(s), whisked with the mustard until foamy; and one for the pretzel crumbs.

3. Dip a section of pork tenderloin in the egg white mixture and turn it to coat well, even on the ends. Let any excess egg white mixture slip back into the rest, then set the pork in the pretzel crumbs. Roll it several times, pressing gently, until the pork is evenly coated, even on the ends. Generously coat the pork section with vegetable oil spray, set it aside, and continue coating and spraying the remaining sections.

4. Set the pork sections in the air fryer oven with at least ¼ inch between them. Air-fry undisturbed for 10 minutes, or until an instant-read meat thermometer inserted into the center of one section registers 145°F.

5. Use kitchen tongs to transfer the pieces to a wire rack. Cool for 3 to 5 minutes before serving.

Barbecued Broiled Pork Chops

Servings: 2

Cooking Time: 16 Minutes

Ingredients:

- Barbecue sauce mixture:
- 1 tablespoon ketchup
- ¼ cup dry red wine
- 1 tablespoon vegetable oil
- ⅛ teaspoon smoked flavoring (liquid smoke)
- 1 teaspoon chili powder
- 1 teaspoon ground cumin
- 1 teaspoon brown sugar
- ¼ teaspoon butcher's pepper
- 2 large (6- to 8-ounce) lean pork chops, approximately ¾ to 1 inch thick

Directions:

1. Combine the barbecue sauce mixture ingredients in a small bowl. Brush the chops with the sauce and place on a broiling rack with a pan underneath.

2. BROIL 8 minutes, turn with tongs, and broil for another 8 minutes, or until the meat is cooked to your preference.

Lime-ginger Pork Tenderloin

Servings: 4

Cooking Time: 26 Minutes

Ingredients:

- ½ cup packed dark brown sugar
- Juice of ½ lime
- 2 teaspoons fresh ginger, peeled and grated
- 1 teaspoon minced garlic
- 2 (1-pound) extra-lean pork tenderloins, trimmed of fat
- Sea salt, for seasoning
- Freshly ground black pepper, for seasoning
- 1 tablespoon olive oil

Directions:

1. Preheat the toaster oven to 400°F on CONVECTION BAKE for 5 minutes.
2. In a small bowl, stir the sugar, lime juice, ginger, and garlic together.
3. Lightly season the pork tenderloins all over with salt and pepper.
4. Heat the oil in a large skillet over medium-high heat. Brown the pork on all sides, about 6 minutes in total.
5. Place the air-fryer basket in the baking tray and place the tenderloins in the basket.
6. Brush the pork all over with the ginger-lime mixture.
7. In position 2, bake for 20 minutes, basting the pork at 10 minutes, until it reaches an internal temperature of about 145°F.
8. Let the pork rest for 10 minutes and serve.

Pork Taco Gorditas

Servings: 4

Cooking Time: 21 Minutes

Ingredients:

- 1 pound lean ground pork
- 2 tablespoons chili powder
- 2 tablespoons ground cumin
- 1 teaspoon dried oregano
- 2 teaspoons paprika
- 1 teaspoon garlic powder
- ½ cup water
- 1 (15-ounce) can pinto beans, drained and rinsed
- ½ cup taco sauce
- salt and freshly ground black pepper
- 2 cups grated Cheddar cheese
- 5 (12-inch) flour tortillas
- 4 (8-inch) crispy corn tortilla shells
- 4 cups shredded lettuce
- 1 tomato, diced
- ⅓ cup sliced black olives
- sour cream, for serving
- tomato salsa, for serving

Directions:

1. Preheat the toaster oven to 400°F.

2. Place the ground pork in the air fryer oven and air-fry at 400°F for 10 minutes, stirring a few times during the cooking process to gently break up the meat. Combine the chili powder, cumin, oregano, paprika, garlic powder and water in a small bowl. Stir the spice mixture into the browned pork. Stir in the beans and taco sauce and air-fry for an additional minute. Transfer the pork mixture to a bowl. Season to taste with salt and freshly ground black pepper.

3. Sprinkle ½ cup of the shredded cheese in the center of four of the flour tortillas, making sure to leave a 2-inch border around the edge free of cheese and filling. Divide the pork mixture among the four tortillas, placing it on top of the cheese. Place a crunchy corn tortilla on top of the pork and top with shredded lettuce, diced tomatoes, and black olives. Cut the remaining flour tortilla into 4 quarters. These quarters of tortilla will serve as the bottom of the gordita. Place one quarter tortilla on top of each gordita and fold the edges of the bottom flour tortilla up over the sides, enclosing the filling. While holding the seams down, brush the bottom of the gordita with olive oil and place the seam side down on the countertop while you finish the remaining three gorditas.

4. Preheat the toaster oven to 380°F.

5. Air-fry one gordita at a time. Transfer the gordita carefully to the air fryer oven, seam side down. Brush or spray the top tortilla with oil and air-fry for 5 minutes. Carefully turn the gordita over and air-fry for an additional 5 minutes, until both sides are browned. When finished air frying all four gorditas, layer them back into the air fryer oven for an additional minute to make sure they are all warm before serving with sour cream and salsa.

Italian Sausage & Peppers

Servings: 6

Cooking Time: 25 Minutes

Ingredients:

- 1 6-ounce can tomato paste
- ⅔ cup water
- 1 8-ounce can tomato sauce
- 1 teaspoon dried parsley flakes
- ½ teaspoon garlic powder
- ⅛ teaspoon oregano
- ½ pound mild Italian bulk sausage
- 1 tablespoon extra virgin olive oil
- ½ large onion, cut in 1-inch chunks
- 4 ounces fresh mushrooms, sliced
- 1 large green bell pepper, cut in 1-inch chunks
- 8 ounces spaghetti, cooked
- Parmesan cheese for serving

Directions:

1. In a large saucepan or skillet, stir together the tomato paste, water, tomato sauce, parsley, garlic, and oregano. Heat on stovetop over very low heat while preparing meat and vegetables.

2. Break sausage into small chunks, about ½-inch pieces. Place in air fryer oven baking pan.

3. Air-fry at 390°F for 5 minutes. Stir. Cook 7 minutes longer or until sausage is well done. Remove from pan, drain on paper towels, and add to the sauce mixture.

4. If any sausage grease remains in baking pan, pour it off or use paper towels to soak it up. (Be careful handling that hot pan!)

5. Place olive oil, onions, and mushrooms in pan and stir. Air-fry for 5 minutes or just until tender. Using a slotted spoon, transfer onions and mushrooms from baking pan into the sauce and sausage mixture.

6. Place bell pepper chunks in air fryer oven baking pan and air-fry for 8 minutes or until tender. When done, stir into sauce with sausage and other vegetables.

7. Serve over cooked spaghetti with plenty of Parmesan cheese.

Almond And Sun-dried Tomato Crusted Pork Chops

Servings: 4

Cooking Time: 10 Minutes

Ingredients:

- ½ cup oil-packed sun-dried tomatoes
- ½ cup toasted almonds
- ¼ cup grated Parmesan cheese
- ½ cup olive oil
- 2 tablespoons water
- ½ teaspoon salt
- freshly ground black pepper
- 4 center-cut boneless pork chops (about 1¼ pounds)

Directions:

1. Place the sun-dried tomatoes into a food processor and pulse them until they are coarsely chopped. Add the almonds, Parmesan cheese, olive oil, water, salt and pepper. Process all the ingredients into a smooth paste. Spread most of the paste (leave a little in reserve) onto both sides of the pork chops and then pierce the meat several times with a needle-style meat tenderizer or a fork. Let the pork chops sit and marinate for at least 1 hour (refrigerate if marinating for longer than 1 hour).

2. Preheat the toaster oven to 370°F.

3. Brush a little olive oil on the bottom of the air fryer oven. Transfer the pork chops into the air fryer oven, spooning a little more of the sun-dried tomato paste onto the pork chops if there are any gaps where the paste may have been rubbed off. Air-fry the pork chops at 370°F for 10 minutes, turning the chops over halfway through the cooking process.

4. When the pork chops have finished cooking, transfer them to a serving plate and serve with mashed potatoes and vegetables for a hearty meal.

POULTRY

Coconut Chicken With Apricot-ginger Sauce

Servings: 4

Cooking Time: 8 Minutes

Ingredients:

- 1½ pounds boneless, skinless chicken tenders, cut in large chunks (about 1¼ inches)
- salt and pepper
- ½ cup cornstarch
- 2 eggs
- 1 tablespoon milk
- 3 cups shredded coconut (see below)
- oil for misting or cooking spray
- Apricot-Ginger Sauce
- ½ cup apricot preserves
- 2 tablespoons white vinegar
- ¼ teaspoon ground ginger
- ¼ teaspoon low-sodium soy sauce
- 2 teaspoons white or yellow onion, grated or finely minced

Directions:

1. Mix all ingredients for the Apricot-Ginger Sauce well and let sit for flavors to blend while you cook the chicken.
2. Season chicken chunks with salt and pepper to taste.
3. Place cornstarch in a shallow dish.
4. In another shallow dish, beat together eggs and milk.
5. Place coconut in a third shallow dish. (If also using panko breadcrumbs, as suggested below, stir them to mix well.)
6. Spray air fryer oven with oil or cooking spray.
7. Dip each chicken chunk into cornstarch, shake off excess, and dip in egg mixture.
8. Shake off excess egg mixture and roll lightly in coconut or coconut mixture. Spray with oil.
9. Place coated chicken chunks in air fryer oven in a single layer, close together but without sides touching.
10. Air-fry at 360°F for 4 minutes, stop, and turn chunks over.
11. Cook an additional 4 minutes or until chicken is done inside and coating is crispy brown.
12. Repeat steps 9 through 11 to cook remaining chicken chunks.

Turkey Sausage Cassoulet

Servings: 4

Cooking Time: 52 Minutes

Ingredients:

- 3 turkey sausages
- 1 teaspoon olive oil
- ½ sweet onion
- 2 celery stalks, chopped
- 1 teaspoon minced garlic
- 2 (15-ounce) cans great northern beans, drained and rinsed
- 1(15-ounce) can fire-roasted tomatoes
- 1 small sweet potato, diced
- 1 teaspoon dried thyme
- 2 cups kale, chopped
- Sea salt, for seasoning
- Freshly ground black pepper, for seasoning

Directions:

1. Preheat the toaster oven to 375°F on AIR FRY for 5 minutes.
2. Place the air-fryer basket in the baking tray and place the sausages in the basket. Prick them all over with a fork.
3. In position 2, air fry for 12 minutes until cooked through. Set the sausages aside to cool until you can handle them. Then cut into ¼-inch slices.
4. Change the oven to BAKE at 375°F and place the rack in position 1.
5. Heat the oil in a small skillet over medium-high heat and sauté the onion, celery, and garlic until softened.
6. Transfer the cooked vegetables to a 1½-quart casserole dish and stir in the sausage, beans, tomatoes, sweet potato, and thyme. Cover with foil or a lid.
7. Bake for 35 to 40 minutes until tender and any liquid is absorbed. Take the casserole out and stir in the kale. Let it sit for 10 minutes to wilt.
8. Season with salt and pepper, and serve.

Chicken-fried Steak With Gravy

Servings: 2

Cooking Time: 16 Minutes

Ingredients:

- FOR THE STEAK
- Oil spray (hand-pumped)
- 1 cup all-purpose flour
- 1 teaspoon garlic powder
- 1 teaspoon onion powder
- 1 teaspoon smoked paprika
- 2 large eggs
- 2 (½-pound) cube steaks
- Sea salt, for seasoning
- Freshly ground black pepper, for seasoning
- FOR THE GRAVY
- 2 tablespoons salted butter
- 2 tablespoons all-purpose flour
- 1½ cups whole milk
- ¼ cup heavy (whipping) cream
- Sea salt, for seasoning
- Freshly ground black pepper, for seasoning

Directions:

1. To make the steak
2. Preheat the toaster oven to 400°F on AIR FRY for 5 minutes.
3. Place the air-fryer basket in the baking tray and spray it generously with the oil.
4. In a medium bowl, stir the flour, garlic powder, onion powder, and paprika until well blended.
5. In a medium bowl, beat the eggs and place them next to the flour.
6. Season the steaks all over with salt and pepper.
7. Dredge a steak in the egg and then in the flour mixture, making sure it is well coated. Shake off any excess flour.
8. Place the steak in the basket and repeat the process with the other steak.
9. Spray the tops of the steaks with the oil.
10. In position 2, air fry for 9 minutes until golden brown and crispy. Turn the steaks over, spray the second side with the oil, and air fry for an additional 7 minutes.
11. Set the steaks aside to rest for 5 minutes.
12. To make the gravy
13. While the steak is air frying, melt the butter in a medium saucepan over medium-high heat.
14. Whisk in the flour and cook for 2 minutes until lightly browned.
15. Whisk in the milk until the gravy is creamy and thick, about 5 minutes. Whisk in the cream and season with salt and pepper.
16. Serve the steak topped with the gravy.

Air-fried Turkey Breast With Cherry Glaze

Servings: 6

Cooking Time: 54 Minutes

Ingredients:

- 1 (5-pound) turkey breast
- 2 teaspoons olive oil
- 1 teaspoon dried thyme
- ½ teaspoon dried sage
- 1 teaspoon salt
- ½ teaspoon freshly ground black pepper
- ½ cup cherry preserves
- 1 tablespoon chopped fresh thyme leaves
- 1 teaspoon soy sauce
- freshly ground black pepper

Directions:

1. All turkeys are built differently, so depending on the turkey breast and how your butcher has prepared it, you may need to trim the bottom of the ribs in order to get the turkey to sit upright in the air fryer oven without touching the heating element. The key to this recipe is getting the right size turkey breast. Once you've managed that, the rest is easy, so make sure your turkey breast fits into the air fryer oven before you Preheat the toaster oven oven.

2. Preheat the toaster oven to 350°F.

3. Brush the turkey breast all over with the olive oil. Combine the thyme, sage, salt and pepper and rub the outside of the turkey breast with the spice mixture.

4. Transfer the seasoned turkey breast to the air fryer oven, breast side up, and air-fry at 350°F for 25 minutes. Turn the turkey breast on its side and air-fry for another 12 minutes. Turn the turkey breast on the opposite side and air-fry for 12 more minutes. The internal temperature of the turkey breast should reach 165°F when fully cooked.

5. While the turkey is air-frying, make the glaze by combining the cherry preserves, fresh thyme, soy sauce and pepper in a small bowl. When the cooking time is up, return the turkey breast to an upright position and brush the glaze all over the turkey. Air-fry for a final 5 minutes, until the skin is nicely browned and crispy. Let the turkey rest, loosely tented with foil, for at least 5 minutes before slicing and serving.

Chicken Parmesan

Ingredients:

- 4 chicken tenders
- Italian seasoning
- salt
- ¼ cup cornstarch
- ½ cup Italian salad dressing
- ¼ cup panko breadcrumbs
- ¼ cup grated Parmesan cheese, plus more for serving
- oil for misting or cooking spray
- 8 ounces spaghetti, cooked
- 1 24-ounce jar marinara sauce

Directions:

1. Pound chicken tenders with meat mallet or rolling pin until about ¼-inch thick.
2. Sprinkle both sides with Italian seasoning and salt to taste.
3. Place cornstarch and salad dressing in 2 separate shallow dishes.
4. In a third shallow dish, mix together the panko crumbs and Parmesan cheese.
5. Dip flattened chicken in cornstarch, then salad dressing. Dip in the panko mixture, pressing into the chicken so the coating sticks well.
6. Spray both sides with oil or cooking spray. Place in air fryer oven in single layer.
7. Air-fry at 390°F for 5 minutes. Spray with oil again, turning chicken to coat both sides. See tip about turning.
8. Air-fry for an additional 6 minutes or until chicken juices run clear and outside is browned.
9. While chicken is cooking, heat marinara sauce and stir into cooked spaghetti.
10. To serve, divide spaghetti with sauce among 4 dinner plates, and top each with a fried chicken tender. Pass additional Parmesan at the table for those who want extra cheese.

Italian Roasted Chicken Thighs

Servings: 6

Cooking Time: 14 Minutes

Ingredients:

- 6 boneless chicken thighs
- ½ teaspoon dried oregano
- ½ teaspoon garlic powder
- ½ teaspoon sea salt
- ½ teaspoon black pepper
- ¼ teaspoon crushed red pepper flakes

Directions:

1. Pat the chicken thighs with paper towel.

2. In a small bowl, mix the oregano, garlic powder, salt, pepper, and crushed red pepper flakes. Rub the spice mixture onto the chicken thighs.

3. Preheat the toaster oven to 400°F.

4. Place the chicken thighs in the air fryer oven and spray with cooking spray. Air-fry for 10 minutes, turn over, and cook another 4 minutes. When cooking completes, the internal temperature should read 165°F.

Marinated Green Pepper And Pineapple Chicken

Servings: 4

Cooking Time: 20 Minutes

Ingredients:

- Marinade:
- 1 teaspoon finely chopped fresh ginger
- 2 garlic cloves, finely chopped
- 1 teaspoon toasted sesame oil
- 1 tablespoon brown sugar
- 2 tablespoons soy sauce
- ¾ cup dry white wine
- 2 skinless, boneless chicken breasts, cut into 1 × 3-inch strips
- 2 tablespoons chopped onion
- 1 bell pepper, chopped
- 1 5-ounce can pineapple chunks, drained
- 2 tablespoons grated unsweetened coconut

Directions:

1. Combine the marinade ingredients in a medium bowl and blend well. Add the chicken strips and spoon the mixture over them. Marinate in the refrigerator for at least 1 hour. Remove the strips from the marinade and place in an oiled or nonstick 8½ × 8½ × 2-inch square (cake) pan. Add the onion and pepper and mix well.

2. BROIL for 8 minutes. Then remove from the oven and, using tongs, turn the chicken, pepper, and onion pieces. (Spoon the reserved marinade over the pieces, if desired.)

3. BROIL again for 8 minutes, or until the chicken, pepper, and onion are cooked through and tender. Add the pineapple chunks and coconut and toss to mix well.

4. BROIL for another 4 minutes, or until the coconut is lightly browned.

Harissa Lemon Whole Chicken

Servings: 6
Cooking Time: 60 Minutes

Ingredients:
- 2 teaspoons kosher salt
- ½ teaspoon freshly ground black pepper
- ½ teaspoon ground cumin
- 2 garlic cloves
- 6 tablespoons harissa paste
- ½ lemon, juiced
- 1 whole lemon, zested
- 1 (5 pound) whole chicken

Directions:
1. Place salt, pepper, cumin, garlic cloves, harissa paste, lemon juice, and lemon zest in a food processor and pulse until they form a smooth puree.
2. Rub the puree all over the chicken, especially inside the cavity, and cover with plastic wrap.
3. Marinate for 1 hour at room temperature.
4. Preheat the toaster oven to 350°F.
5. Place the marinated chicken on the food tray, then insert the tray at low position in the preheated oven.
6. Select the Roast function, then press Start/Pause.
7. Remove when done, tent chicken with foil, and allow it to rest for 20 minutes before serving.

Mediterranean Stuffed Chicken Breasts

Servings: 4

Cooking Time: 24 Minutes

Ingredients:

- 4 boneless, skinless chicken breasts
- ½ teaspoon salt
- ½ teaspoon black pepper
- ½ teaspoon garlic powder
- ½ teaspoon paprika
- ½ cup canned artichoke hearts, chopped
- 4 ounces cream cheese
- ¼ cup grated Parmesan cheese

Directions:

1. Pat the chicken breasts with a paper towel. Using a sharp knife, cut a pouch in the side of each chicken breast for filling.

2. In a small bowl, mix the salt, pepper, garlic powder, and paprika. Season the chicken breasts with this mixture.

3. In a medium bowl, mix together the artichokes, cream cheese, and grated Parmesan cheese. Divide the filling between the 4 breasts, stuffing it inside the pouches. Use toothpicks to close the pouches and secure the filling.

4. Preheat the toaster oven to 360°F.

5. Spray the air fryer oven liberally with cooking spray, add the stuffed chicken breasts to the air fryer oven, and spray liberally with cooking spray again. Air-fry for 14 minutes, carefully turn over the chicken breasts, and cook another 10 minutes. Check the temperature at 20 minutes cooking. Chicken breasts are fully cooked when the center measures 165°F. Cook in batches, if needed.

Chicken Schnitzel Dogs

Servings: 4

Cooking Time: 10 Minutes

Ingredients:

- ½ cup flour
- ½ teaspoon salt
- 1 teaspoon marjoram
- 1 teaspoon dried parsley flakes
- ½ teaspoon thyme
- 1 egg
- 1 teaspoon lemon juice
- 1 teaspoon water
- 1 cup breadcrumbs
- 4 chicken tenders, pounded thin
- oil for misting or cooking spray
- 4 whole-grain hotdog buns
- 4 slices Gouda cheese
- 1 small Granny Smith apple, thinly sliced
- ½ cup shredded Napa cabbage
- coleslaw dressing

Directions:

1. In a shallow dish, mix together the flour, salt, marjoram, parsley, and thyme.
2. In another shallow dish, beat together egg, lemon juice, and water.
3. Place breadcrumbs in a third shallow dish.
4. Cut each of the flattened chicken tenders in half lengthwise.
5. Dip flattened chicken strips in flour mixture, then egg wash. Let excess egg drip off and roll in breadcrumbs. Spray both sides with oil or cooking spray.
6. Air-fry at 390°F for 5 minutes. Spray with oil, turn over, and spray other side.
7. Air-fry for 3 to 5 minutes more, until well done and crispy brown.
8. To serve, place 2 schnitzel strips on bottom of each hot dog bun. Top with cheese, sliced apple, and cabbage. Drizzle with coleslaw dressing and top with other half of bun.

Parmesan Crusted Chicken Cordon Bleu

Servings: 2

Cooking Time: 14 Minutes

Ingredients:

- 2 (6-ounce) boneless, skinless chicken breasts
- salt and freshly ground black pepper
- 1 tablespoon Dijon mustard
- 4 slices Swiss cheese
- 4 slices deli-sliced ham
- ¼ cup all-purpose flour
- 1 egg, beaten
- ¾ cup panko breadcrumbs
- ⅓ cup grated Parmesan cheese
- olive oil, in a spray bottle

Directions:

1. Butterfly the chicken breasts. Place the chicken breast on a cutting board and press down on the breast with the palm of your hand. Slice into the long side of the chicken breast, parallel to the cutting board, but not all the way through to the other side. Open the chicken breast like a "book". Place a piece of plastic wrap over the chicken breast and gently pound it with a meat mallet to make it evenly thick.

2. Season the chicken with salt and pepper. Spread the Dijon mustard on the inside of each chicken breast. Layer one slice of cheese on top of the mustard, then top with the 2 slices of ham and the other slice of cheese.

3. Starting with the long edge of the chicken breast, roll the chicken up to the other side. Secure it shut with 1 or 2 toothpicks.

4. Preheat the toaster oven to 350°F.

5. Set up a dredging station with three shallow dishes. Place the flour in the first dish. Place the beaten egg in the second shallow dish. Combine the panko breadcrumbs and Parmesan cheese together in the third shallow dish. Dip the stuffed and rolled chicken breasts in the flour, then the beaten egg and then roll in the breadcrumb-cheese mixture to cover on all sides. Press the crumbs onto the chicken breasts with your hands to make sure they are well adhered. Spray the chicken breasts with olive oil and transfer to the air fryer oven.

6. Air-fry at 350°F for 14 minutes, flipping the breasts over halfway through the cooking time. Let the chicken rest for a few minutes before removing the toothpicks, slicing and serving.

Poblano Bake

Servings: 4
Cooking Time: 11 Minutes

Ingredients:

- 2 large poblano peppers (approx. 5½ inches long excluding stem)
- ¾ pound ground turkey, raw
- ¾ cup cooked brown rice
- 1 teaspoon chile powder
- ½ teaspoon ground cumin
- ½ teaspoon garlic powder
- 4 ounces sharp Cheddar cheese, grated
- 1 8-ounce jar salsa, warmed

Directions:

1. Slice each pepper in half lengthwise so that you have four wide, flat pepper halves.
2. Remove seeds and membrane and discard. Rinse inside and out.
3. In a large bowl, combine turkey, rice, chile powder, cumin, and garlic powder. Mix well.
4. Divide turkey filling into 4 portions and stuff one into each of the 4 pepper halves. Press lightly to pack down.
5. Place 2 pepper halves in air fryer oven and air-fry at 390°F for 10 minutes or until turkey is well done.
6. Top each pepper half with ¼ of the grated cheese. Cook 1 more minute or just until cheese melts.
7. Repeat steps 5 and 6 to cook remaining pepper halves.
8. To serve, place each pepper half on a plate and top with ¼ cup warm salsa.

Chicken Pot Pie

Servings: 4

Cooking Time: 65 Minutes

Ingredients:

- ¼ cup salted butter
- 1 small sweet onion, chopped
- 1 carrot, chopped
- 1 teaspoon minced garlic
- ¼ cup all-purpose flour
- 1 cup low-sodium chicken broth
- ¼ cup heavy (whipping) cream
- 2 cups diced store-bought rotisserie chicken
- 1 cup frozen peas
- Sea salt, for seasoning
- Freshly ground black pepper, for seasoning
- 1 unbaked store-bought pie crust

Directions:

1. Place the rack in position 1 and preheat the toaster oven to 350°F on BAKE for 5 minutes.
2. Melt the butter in a large saucepan over medium-high heat. Sauté the onion, carrot, and garlic until softened, about 12 minutes. Whisk in the flour to form a thick paste and whisk for 1 minute to cook.
3. Add the broth and whisk until thickened, about 2 minutes. Add the heavy cream, whisking to combine. Add the chicken and peas, and season with salt and pepper.
4. Transfer the filling to a 1½-quart casserole dish and top with the pie crust, tucking the edges into the sides of the casserole dish to completely enclose the filling. Cut 4 or 5 slits in the top of the crust.
5. Bake for 50 minutes until the crust is golden brown and the filling is bubbly. Serve.

Gluten-free Nutty Chicken Fingers

Servings: 4

Cooking Time: 10 Minutes

Ingredients:

- ½ cup gluten-free flour
- ½ teaspoon garlic powder
- ¼ teaspoon onion powder
- ¼ teaspoon black pepper
- ¼ teaspoon salt
- 1 cup walnuts, pulsed into coarse flour
- ½ cup gluten-free breadcrumbs
- 2 large eggs
- 1 pound boneless, skinless chicken tenders

Directions:

1. Preheat the toaster oven to 400°F.
2. In a medium bowl, mix the flour, garlic, onion, pepper, and salt. Set aside.
3. In a separate bowl, mix the walnut flour and breadcrumbs.
4. In a third bowl, whisk the eggs.
5. Liberally spray the air fryer oven with olive oil spray.
6. Pat the chicken tenders dry with a paper towel. Dredge the tenders one at a time in the flour, then dip them in the egg, and toss them in the breadcrumb coating. Repeat until all tenders are coated.
7. Set each tender in the air fryer oven, leaving room on each side of the tender to allow for flipping.
8. When the air fryer oven is full, cook 5 minutes, flip, and cook another 5 minutes. Check the internal temperature after cooking completes; it should read 165°F. If it does not, cook another 2 to 4 minutes.
9. Remove the tenders and let cool 5 minutes before serving. Repeat until all the tenders are cooked.

Oven-crisped Chicken

Servings: 4

Cooking Time: 35 Minutes

Ingredients:

- Coating mixture:
- 1 cup cornmeal
- ¼ cup wheat germ
- 1 teaspoon paprika
- 1 teaspoon garlic powder
- Salt and butcher's pepper to taste
- 3 tablespoons olive oil
- 1 tablespoon spicy brown mustard
- 6 skinless, boneless chicken thighs

Directions:

1. Preheat the toaster oven to 375° F.

2. Combine the coating mixture ingredients in a small bowl and transfer to a plate, spreading the mixture evenly over the plate's surface. Set aside.

3. Whisk together the oil and mustard in a bowl. Add the chicken pieces and toss to coat thoroughly. Press both sides of each piece into the coating mixture to coat well. Chill in the refrigerator for 10 minutes. Transfer the chicken pieces to a broiling rack with a pan underneath.

4. BAKE, uncovered, for 35 minutes, or until the meat is tender and the coating is crisp and golden brown or browned to your preference.

Quick Chicken For Filling

Servings: 2

Cooking Time: 8 Minutes

Ingredients:

- 1 pound chicken tenders, skinless and boneless
- ½ teaspoon ground cumin
- ½ teaspoon garlic powder
- cooking spray

Directions:

1. Sprinkle raw chicken tenders with seasonings.

2. Spray air fryer oven lightly with cooking spray to prevent sticking.

3. Place chicken in air fryer oven in single layer.

4. Air-fry at 390°F for 4 minutes, turn chicken strips over, and air-fry for an additional 4 minutes.

5. Test for doneness. Thick tenders may require an additional minute or two.

Sesame Chicken Breasts

Servings: 2
Cooking Time: 20 Minutes

Ingredients:

- Mixture:
- 2 tablespoons sesame oil
- 2 teaspoons soy sauce
- 2 teaspoons balsamic vinegar
- 2 skinless, boneless chicken breast filets
- 3 tablespoons sesame seeds

Directions:

1. Combine the mixture ingredients in a small bowl and brush the filets liberally. Reserve the mixture. Place the filets on a broiling rack with a pan underneath.

2. BROIL 15 minutes, or until the meat is tender and the juices, when the meat is pierced, run clear. Remove from the oven and brush the filets with the remaining mixture. Place the sesame seeds on a plate and press the chicken breast halves into the seeds, coating well.

3. BROIL for 5 minutes, or until the sesame seeds are browned.

Southwest Gluten-free Turkey Meatloaf

Servings: 8

Cooking Time: 35 Minutes

Ingredients:

- 1 pound lean ground turkey
- ¼ cup corn grits
- ¼ cup diced onion
- 1 teaspoon minced garlic
- ½ teaspoon black pepper
- ½ teaspoon salt
- 1 large egg
- ½ cup ketchup
- 4 teaspoons chipotle hot sauce
- ⅓ cup shredded cheddar cheese

Directions:

1. Preheat the toaster oven to 350°F.
2. In a large bowl, mix together the ground turkey, corn grits, onion, garlic, black pepper, and salt.
3. In a small bowl, whisk the egg. Add the egg to the turkey mixture and combine.
4. In a small bowl, mix the ketchup and hot sauce. Set aside.
5. Liberally spray a 9-x-4-inch loaf pan with olive oil spray. Depending on the size of your air fryer oven, you may need to use 2 or 3 mini loaf pans.
6. Spoon the ground turkey mixture into the loaf pan and evenly top with half of the ketchup mixture. Cover with foil and place the meatloaf into the air fryer oven. Air-fry for 30 minutes; remove the foil and discard. Check the internal temperature (it should be nearing 165°F).
7. Coat the top of the meatloaf with the remaining ketchup mixture, and sprinkle the cheese over the top. Place the meatloaf back in the air fryer oven for the remaining 5 minutes (or until the internal temperature reaches 165°F).
8. Remove from the oven and let cool 5 minutes before serving. Serve warm with desired sides.

VEGETABLES AND VEGETARIAN

Steakhouse Baked Potatoes

Servings: 3

Cooking Time: 55 Minutes

Ingredients:

- 3 10-ounce russet potatoes
- 2 tablespoons Olive oil
- 1 teaspoon Table salt

Directions:

1. Preheat the toaster oven to 375°F .

2. Poke holes all over each potato with a fork. Rub the skin of each potato with 2 teaspoons of the olive oil, then sprinkle ¼ teaspoon salt all over each potato.

3. When the machine is at temperature, set the potatoes in the air fryer oven in one layer with as much air space between them as possible. Air-fry for 50 minutes, turning once, or until soft to the touch but with crunchy skins. If the machine is at 360°F, you may need to add up to 5 minutes to the cooking time.

4. Use kitchen tongs to gently transfer the baked potatoes to a wire rack. Cool for 5 or 10 minutes before serving.

Wilted Brussels Sprout Slaw

Servings: 4

Cooking Time: 18 Minutes

Ingredients:

- 2 Thick-cut bacon strip(s), halved widthwise (gluten-free, if a concern)
- 4½ cups (about 1 pound 2 ounces) Bagged shredded Brussels sprouts
- ¼ teaspoon Table salt
- 2 tablespoons White balsamic vinegar
- 2 teaspoons Worcestershire sauce (gluten-free, if a concern)
- 1 teaspoon Dijon mustard (gluten-free, if a concern)
- ¼ teaspoon Ground black pepper

Directions:

1. Preheat the toaster oven to 375°F .

2. When the machine is at temperature, lay the bacon strip halves in the air fryer oven in one layer and air-fry for 10 minutes, or until crisp.

3. Use kitchen tongs to transfer the bacon pieces to a wire rack. Put the shredded Brussels sprouts in a large bowl. Drain any fat from the pan or the tray under the pan onto the Brussels sprouts. Add the salt and toss well to coat.

4. Put the Brussels sprout shreds in the air fryer oven, spreading them out into as close to an even layer as you can. Air-fry for 8 minutes, tossing the air fryer oven's contents at least three times, until wilted and lightly browned.

5. Pour the contents of the air fryer oven into a serving bowl. Chop the bacon and add it to the Brussels sprouts. Add the vinegar, Worcestershire sauce, mustard, and pepper. Toss well to blend the dressing and coat the Brussels sprout shreds. Serve warm.

Blistered Green Beans

Servings: 3

Cooking Time: 10 Minutes

Ingredients:

- ¾ pound Green beans, trimmed on both ends
- 1½ tablespoons Olive oil
- 3 tablespoons Pine nuts
- 1½ tablespoons Balsamic vinegar
- 1½ teaspoons Minced garlic
- ¾ teaspoon Table salt
- ¾ teaspoon Ground black pepper

Directions:

1. Preheat the toaster oven to 400°F.

2. Toss the green beans and oil in a large bowl until all the green beans are glistening.

3. When the machine is at temperature, pile the green beans into the air fryer oven. Air-fry for 10 minutes, tossing often to rearrange the green beans in the air fryer oven, or until blistered and tender.

4. Dump the contents of the air fryer oven into a serving bowl. Add the pine nuts, vinegar, garlic, salt, and pepper. Toss well to coat and combine. Serve warm or at room temperature.

Roasted Ratatouille Vegetables

Servings: 15

Cooking Time: 2 Minutes

Ingredients:

- 1 baby or Japanese eggplant, cut into 1½-inch cubes
- 1 red pepper, cut into 1-inch chunks
- 1 yellow pepper, cut into 1-inch chunks
- 1 zucchini, cut into 1-inch chunks
- 1 clove garlic, minced
- ½ teaspoon dried basil
- 1 tablespoon olive oil
- salt and freshly ground black pepper
- ¼ cup sliced sun-dried tomatoes in oil
- 2 tablespoons chopped fresh basil

Directions:

1. Preheat the toaster oven to 400°F.

2. Toss the eggplant, peppers and zucchini with the garlic, dried basil, olive oil, salt and freshly ground black pepper.

3. Air-fry the vegetables at 400°F for 15 minutes.

4. As soon as the vegetables are tender, toss them with the sliced sun-dried tomatoes and fresh basil and serve.

Classic Falafel

Servings: 4

Cooking Time: 14 Minutes

Ingredients:

- 1 (15-ounce) can low-sodium chickpeas, drained and rinsed
- 3 shallots, roughly chopped
- 3 tablespoons chickpea flour
- ¼ cup fresh parsley, roughly chopped
- 2 tablespoons cilantro, chopped
- 2 teaspoons minced garlic
- 1 teaspoon ground coriander
- 1 teaspoon ground cumin
- ½ teaspoon sea salt
- ⅛ teaspoon allspice
- Oil spray (hand-pumped)

Directions:

1. Preheat the toaster oven to 350°F on AIR FRY for 5 minutes.
2. Place the chickpeas in a food processor and pulse until roughly chopped.
3. Add the shallots, flour, parsley, cilantro, garlic, coriander, cumin, salt, and allspice, and pulse to form a thick paste.
4. Roll the chickpea mixture into 2-inch balls and flatten them slightly with the palm of your hand.
5. Place the air-fryer basket in the baking tray and coat it generously with oil spray.
6. Place the falafel in a single layer in the basket. Spray the patties with oil on both sides. You might have to work in batches.
7. Place the tray in position 2 and air fry until golden, turning halfway through, for about 14 minutes in total. Repeat with remaining patties. Serve.

Roasted Heirloom Carrots With Orange And Thyme

Servings: 2

Cooking Time: 12 Minutes

Ingredients:

- 10 to 12 heirloom or rainbow carrots (about 1 pound), scrubbed but not peeled
- 1 teaspoon olive oil
- salt and freshly ground black pepper
- 1 tablespoon butter
- 1 teaspoon fresh orange zest
- 1 teaspoon chopped fresh thyme

Directions:

1. Preheat the toaster oven to 400°F.
2. Scrub the carrots and halve them lengthwise. Toss them in the olive oil, season with salt and freshly ground black pepper and transfer to the air fryer oven.
3. Air-fry at 400°F for 12 minutes.
4. As soon as the carrots have finished cooking, add the butter, orange zest and thyme and toss all the ingredients together in the air fryer oven to melt the butter and coat evenly. Serve warm.

Golden Grilled Cheese Tomato Sandwich

Servings: 2

Cooking Time: 10 Minutes

Ingredients:

- 4 slices whole-grain bread
- 4 teaspoons salted butter at room temperature, divided
- 4 to 6 slices cheddar cheese, or your favorite cheese
- 1 large tomato, thinly sliced

Directions:

1. Preheat the toaster oven to 350°F on AIR FRY for 5 minutes.
2. Place the air-fryer basket in the baking sheet and set aside.
3. Butter all four pieces of bread, using 1 teaspoon of butter for each and place 2 pieces of bread, butter-side down, in the basket. Evenly divide the cheese between the 2 bread slices and top with tomato slices. Place the remaining 2 pieces of bread on the tomatoes, butter-side up.
4. Place the tray in position 2 and air fry for 5 minutes until golden brown. Flip the sandwiches and air fry until the cheese is melted and the other side of the bread is golden brown, about 5 minutes. Serve.

Air-fried Potato Salad

Servings: 4

Cooking Time: 15 Minutes

Ingredients:

- 1⅓ pounds Yellow potatoes, such as Yukon Golds, cut into ½-inch chunks
- 1 large Sweet white onion(s), such as Vidalia, chopped into ½-inch pieces
- 1 tablespoon plus 2 teaspoons Olive oil
- ¾ cup Thinly sliced celery
- 6 tablespoons Regular or low-fat mayonnaise (gluten-free, if a concern)
- 2½ tablespoons Apple cider vinegar
- 1½ teaspoons Dijon mustard (gluten-free, if a concern)
- ¾ teaspoon Table salt
- ¼ teaspoon Ground black pepper

Directions:

1. Preheat the toaster oven to 400°F.
2. Toss the potatoes, onion(s), and oil in a large bowl until the vegetables are glistening with oil.
3. When the machine is at temperature, transfer the vegetables to the air fryer oven, spreading them out into as even a layer as you can. Air-fry for 15 minutes, tossing and rearranging the vegetables every 3 minutes so that all surfaces get exposed to the air currents, until the vegetables are tender and even browned at the edges.
4. Pour the contents of the air fryer oven into a serving bowl. Cool for at least 5 minutes or up to 30 minutes. Add the celery, mayonnaise, vinegar, mustard, salt, and pepper. Stir well to coat. The potato salad can be made in advance; cover and refrigerate for up to 4 days.

Lentil-stuffed Zucchini

Servings: 2

Cooking Time: 50 Minutes

Ingredients:

- 2 large zucchini
- 2 teaspoons olive oil
- 1 (15-ounce) can low-sodium lentils, drained and rinsed
- 1 large tomato, chopped
- 1 scallion, both white and green parts, chopped
- ½ jalapeño pepper, minced
- ½ cup corn kernels, fresh or frozen (thawed)
- 1 tablespoon fresh cilantro, chopped
- 1 teaspoon minced garlic
- 1 teaspoon ground cumin
- ¼ teaspoon chili powder
- ½ cup shredded Monterey Jack cheese

Directions:

1. Preheat the toaster oven to 400°F on BAKE for 5 minutes.
2. Line the baking tray with parchment paper.
3. Cut the zucchini in half lengthwise and scoop out the insides so that you have a hollow shell (about ¼-inch thick all the way around).
4. Lightly oil both sides of the zucchini shells and set them on the baking sheet.
5. In a large bowl, stir the lentils, tomato, scallion, jalapeño, corn, cilantro, garlic, cumin, and chili powder until well mixed.
6. Spoon the lentil mixture into the zucchini and top with the cheese.
7. Bake for 50 minutes. The zucchini should be tender, the filling heated through, and the cheese melted and lightly browned. Serve.

Ratatouille

Servings: 4
Cooking Time: 60 Minutes

Ingredients:

- Oil spray (hand-pumped)
- 1 eggplant, peeled and diced into ½-inch chunks
- 2 tomatoes, diced
- 1 zucchini, diced
- 2 bell peppers (any color), diced
- ½ red onion, chopped
- ½ cup tomato paste
- 2 teaspoons minced garlic
- 1 teaspoon dried basil
- ¼ teaspoon sea salt
- ⅛ teaspoon freshly ground black pepper
- Pinch red pepper flakes
- ½ cup low-sodium vegetable broth

Directions:

1. Place the rack in position 1 and preheat oven to 350°F on CONVECTION BAKE for 5 minutes.
2. Lightly coat a 1½-quart casserole dish with oil spray.
3. In a large bowl, toss the eggplant, tomatoes, zucchini, bell peppers, onion, tomato paste, garlic, basil, salt, black pepper, and red pepper flakes until well combined.
4. Transfer the vegetable mixture to the casserole dish, pour in the vegetable broth, and cover tightly with foil or a lid.
5. Convection bake for 1 hour, stirring once at the halfway mark, until the vegetables are very tender. Serve.

Parmesan Garlic Fries

Servings: 4
Cooking Time: 20 Minutes

Ingredients:

- 2 medium Yukon gold potatoes, washed
- 1 tablespoon extra-virgin olive oil
- 1 garlic clove, minced
- 2 tablespoons finely grated parmesan cheese
- ¼ teaspoon black pepper
- ¼ teaspoon salt
- 1 tablespoon freshly chopped parsley

Directions:

1. Preheat the toaster oven to 400°F.
2. Slice the potatoes into long strips about ¼-inch thick. In a large bowl, toss the potatoes with the olive oil, garlic, cheese, pepper, and salt.
3. Place the fries into the air fryer oven and air-fry for 8 minutes.
4. Remove and serve warm.

Grits Casserole

Servings: 4
Cooking Time: 30 Minutes

Ingredients:

- 10 fresh asparagus spears, cut into 1-inch pieces
- 2 cups cooked grits, cooled to room temperature
- 1 egg, beaten
- 2 teaspoons Worcestershire sauce
- ½ teaspoon garlic powder
- ¼ teaspoon salt
- 2 slices provolone cheese (about 1½ ounces)
- oil for misting or cooking spray

Directions:

1. Mist asparagus spears with oil and air-fry at 390°F for 5 minutes, until crisp-tender.
2. In a medium bowl, mix together the grits, egg, Worcestershire, garlic powder, and salt.
3. Spoon half of grits mixture into air fryer oven baking pan and top with asparagus.
4. Tear cheese slices into pieces and layer evenly on top of asparagus.
5. Top with remaining grits.
6. Bake at 360°F for 25 minutes. The casserole will rise a little as it cooks. When done, the top will have browned lightly with just a hint of crispiness.

Simple Roasted Sweet Potatoes

Servings: 2
Cooking Time: 45 Minutes

Ingredients:

- 2 10- to 12-ounce sweet potato(es)

Directions:

1. Preheat the toaster oven to 350°F .
2. Prick the sweet potato(es) in four or five different places with the tines of a flatware fork (not in a line but all around).
3. When the machine is at temperature, set the sweet potato(es) in the air fryer oven with as much air space between them as possible. Air-fry undisturbed for 45 minutes, or until soft when pricked with a fork.
4. Use kitchen tongs to transfer the sweet potato(es) to a wire rack. Cool for 5 minutes before serving.

Honey-roasted Parsnips

Servings: 3
Cooking Time: 23 Minutes

Ingredients:
- 1½ pounds Medium parsnips, peeled
- Olive oil spray
- 1 tablespoon Honey
- 1½ teaspoons Water
- ¼ teaspoon Table salt

Directions:
1. Preheat the toaster oven to 350°F .
2. If the thick end of a parsnip is more than ½ inch in diameter, cut the parsnip just below where it swells to its large end, then slice the large section in half lengthwise. Generously coat the parsnips on all sides with olive oil spray.
3. When the machine is at temperature, set the parsnips in the air fryer oven with as much air space between them as possible. Air-fry undisturbed for 20 minutes.
4. Whisk the honey, water, and salt in a small bowl until smooth. Brush this mixture over the parsnips. Air-fry undisturbed for 3 minutes more, or until the glaze is lightly browned.
5. Use kitchen tongs to transfer the parsnips to a wire rack or a serving platter. Cool for a couple of minutes before serving.

Street Corn

Servings: 4
Cooking Time: 10 Minutes

Ingredients:
- 1 tablespoon butter
- 4 ears corn
- ⅓ cup plain Greek yogurt
- 2 tablespoons Parmesan cheese
- ½ teaspoon paprika
- ½ teaspoon garlic powder
- ¼ teaspoon salt
- ¼ teaspoon black pepper
- ¼ cup finely chopped cilantro

Directions:
1. Preheat the toaster oven to 400°F.
2. In a medium microwave-safe bowl, melt the butter in the microwave. Lightly brush the outside of the ears of corn with the melted butter.
3. Place the corn into the air fryer oven and air-fry for 5 minutes, flip the corn, and cook another 5 minutes.
4. Meanwhile, in a medium bowl, mix the yogurt, cheese, paprika, garlic powder, salt, and pepper. Set aside.
5. Carefully remove the corn from the air fryer oven and let cool 3 minutes. Brush the outside edges with the yogurt mixture and top with fresh chopped cilantro. Serve immediately.

Vegetable–goat Cheese Flatbreads

Servings: 4

Cooking Time: 17 Minutes

Ingredients:

- 1 (8-inch-wide) rectangular flatbread
- ½ cup store-bought sun-dried tomato pesto
- 12 thin zucchini slices
- ¼ cup mushrooms, thinly sliced
- ¼ red onion, thinly sliced
- 1 tomato, chopped
- ¾ cup goat cheese, crumbled

Directions:

1. Line the baking tray with parchment paper. Place the flatbread on the baking tray and TOAST in position 2 for 5 minutes on medium darkness until lightly crisped. Remove from the oven.

2. Preheat the toaster oven to 400°F on BAKE.

3. Spread the pesto on the flatbread, leaving a ½-inch border along the edge. Scatter the zucchini, mushrooms, onion, and tomato evenly on the flatbread. Top with the goat cheese.

4. Place the baking tray in position 2 and bake for 10 to 12 minutes until crispy and the cheese is melted and lightly browned. Serve.

Roasted Garlic

Servings: 1

Cooking Time: 20 Minutes

Ingredients:

- 3 whole garlic buds
- 3 tablespoons olive oil
- Salt and freshly ground black pepper

Directions:

1. Preheat the toaster oven to 450° F.

2. Place the garlic buds in an oiled or nonstick 8½ × 8½ × 2-inch square baking (cake) pan.

3. BAKE, uncovered, for 20 minutes, or until the buds are tender when pierced with a skewer or sharp knife. When cool enough to handle, peel and mash the baked cloves with a fork into the olive oil. Season with salt and pepper to taste.

Cheesy Texas Toast

Servings: 2

Cooking Time: 4 Minutes

Ingredients:

- 2 1-inch-thick slice(s) Italian bread (each about 4 inches across)
- 4 teaspoons Softened butter
- 2 teaspoons Minced garlic
- ¼ cup (about ¾ ounce) Finely grated Parmesan cheese

Directions:

1. Preheat the toaster oven to 400°F.

2. Spread one side of a slice of bread with 2 teaspoons butter. Sprinkle with 1 teaspoon minced garlic, followed by 2 tablespoons grated cheese. Repeat this process if you're making one or more additional toasts.

3. When the machine is at temperature, put the bread slice(s) cheese side up in the air fryer oven (with as much air space between them as possible if you're making more than one). Air-fry undisturbed for 4 minutes, or until browned and crunchy.

4. Use a nonstick-safe spatula to transfer the toasts cheese side up to a wire rack. Cool for 5 minutes before serving.

Yogurt Zucchini With Onion

Servings: 4

Cooking Time: 30 Minutes

Ingredients:

- ½ cup plain fat-free yogurt
- 1 tablespoon unbleached flour
- 4 small zucchini, scrubbed and sliced into ½-inch strips
- 3 tablespoons minced fresh onion
- 1 tablespoon olive oil
- 3 tablespoons pine nuts, ground in a blender
- Salt and freshly ground black pepper

Directions:

1. Preheat the toaster oven to 400° F.

2. Whisk together the yogurt and flour in a small bowl until smooth. Transfer to a 1-quart 8½ × 8½ × 4-inch ovenproof baking dish. Add all the remaining ingredients, mixing well. Adjust the seasonings to taste. Cover the dish with aluminum foil.

3. BAKE, covered, for 25 minutes, or until the zucchini is tender. Uncover and toss gently to blend.

4. BROIL for 5 minutes, or until the top is lightly browned.

DESSERTS

Giant Buttery Oatmeal Cookie

Servings: 4

Cooking Time: 16 Minutes

Ingredients:

- 1 cup Rolled oats (not quick-cooking or steel-cut oats)
- ½ cup All-purpose flour
- ½ teaspoon Baking soda
- ½ teaspoon Ground cinnamon
- ½ teaspoon Table salt
- 3½ tablespoons Butter, at room temperature
- ⅓ cup Packed dark brown sugar
- 1½ tablespoons Granulated white sugar
- 3 tablespoons (or 1 medium egg, well beaten) Pasteurized egg substitute, such as Egg Beaters
- ¾ teaspoon Vanilla extract
- ⅓ cup Chopped pecans
- Baking spray

Directions:

1. Preheat the toaster oven to 350°F.
2. Stir the oats, flour, baking soda, cinnamon, and salt in a bowl until well combined.
3. Using an electric hand mixer at medium speed , beat the butter, brown sugar, and granulated white sugar until creamy and thick, about 3 minutes, scraping down the inside of the bowl occasionally. Beat in the egg substitute or egg (as applicable) and vanilla until uniform.
4. Scrape down and remove the beaters. Fold in the flour mixture and pecans with a rubber spatula just until all the flour is moistened and the nuts are even throughout the dough.
5. For a small air fryer oven, coat the inside of a 6-inch round cake pan with baking spray. For a medium air fryer oven, coat the inside of a 7-inch round cake pan with baking spray. And for a large air fryer oven, coat the inside of an 8-inch round cake pan with baking spray. Scrape and gently press the dough into the prepared pan, spreading it into an even layer to the perimeter.
6. Set the pan in the toaster oven and air-fry undisturbed for 16 minutes, or until puffed and browned.
7. Transfer the pan to a wire rack and cool for 10 minutes. Loosen the cookie from the perimeter with a spatula, then invert the pan onto a cutting board and let the cookie come free. Remove the pan and reinvert the cookie onto the wire rack. Cool for 5 minutes more before slicing into wedges to serve.

Blueberry Cookies

Servings: 4

Cooking Time: 12 Minutes

Ingredients:

- 1 egg
- 1 tablespoon margarine, at room temperature
- ⅓ cup sugar
- 1¼ cups unbleached flour
- Salt to taste
- 1 teaspoon baking powder
- 1 10-ounce package frozen blueberries, well drained, or
- 1½ cups fresh blueberries, rinsed and drained

Directions:

1. Preheat the toaster oven to 400° F.

2. Beat together the egg, margarine, and sugar in a medium bowl with an electric mixer until smooth. Add the flour, salt, and baking powder, mixing thoroughly. Gently stir in the blueberries just to blend. Do not overmix.

3. Drop by teaspoonfuls on an oiled or nonstick 6½ × 10-inch baking sheet or an oiled or nonstick 8½ × 8½ × 2-inch square baking (cake) pan.

4. BAKE for 12 minutes, or until the cookies are golden brown.

Soft Peanut Butter Cookies

Servings: 12

Cooking Time: 20 Minutes

Ingredients:

- 1/2 cup vegetable shortening
- 1/2 cup peanut butter
- 1 1/4 cups light brown sugar
- 1 egg
- 1 teaspoon vanilla
- 1/2 teaspoon salt
- 1 1/2 cups flour
- 1 teaspoon baking soda
- Sugar crystals

Directions:

1. Preheat the toaster oven to 275°F.

2. Using the flat beater attachment, beat shortening, peanut butter, brown sugar, egg, and vanilla at a medium setting until well blended.

3. Reduce speed to low and gradually add dry ingredients until blended. Dough will be crumbly.

4. Roll 3 tablespoon-size portions of the dough into a ball. Place on ungreased cookie sheet.

5. Press to 1/2-inch thick. Sprinkle with sugar crystals.

6. Bake 18 to 20 minutes. Do not overcook.

Orange Almond Ricotta Cookies

Servings: 24

Cooking Time: 15 Minutes

Ingredients:

- Cookie Ingredients
- ½ stick unsalted butter, room temperature
- 1 cup sugar
- 1 large egg
- 1 cup ricotta cheese, drained
- 1½ tablespoons orange juice
- 1 orange, zested
- ¼ teaspoon almond extract
- 1¼ cups all purpose flour
- ½ teaspoon baking powder
- ½ teaspoon salt
- Glaze Ingredients
- 1 cup powdered sugar
- 1½ tablespoons orange juice
- ½ orange, zested

Directions:

1. Beat together the butter and sugar for 3 minutes or until light and fluffy.
2. Add the egg, ricotta, orange juice, orange zest, and almond extract and beat until well combined. Add the flour, baking powder, and salt, then fold gently to combine. Don't overmix.
3. Preheat the toaster Oven to 350°F.
4. Line the food tray with parchment paper, then divide the dough into 1½-tablespoon pieces and place on the tray.
5. Insert the tray at mid position in the preheated oven.
6. Select the Bake function, adjust time to 15 minutes, and press Start/Pause.
7. Remove when done and allow cookies to cool completely before glazing.
8. Make the glaze by stirring together the powdered sugar, orange juice, and zest until smooth. According to your preference, add more powdered sugar to make the glaze thicker, or more orange juice to make the glaze thinner.
9. Spoon about ½-teaspoon of the glaze on each cookie and spread gently. Allow the glaze to harden before serving

Apple Juice Piecrust

Servings: 4
Cooking Time: 10 Minutes

Ingredients:

- 1¼ cups unbleached flour
- ¼ cup margarine
- ¼ cup apple juice
- Pinch of grated nutmeg
- Salt to taste

Directions:

1. Preheat the toaster oven to 350° F.
2. Cut together the flour and margarine with a knife or pastry cutter until the mixture is crumbly. Add the apple juice, nutmeg, and salt and cut again to blend. Turn the dough out onto a lightly floured surface and knead for 2 minutes. Roll out into a circle large enough to fit a 9¾-inch pie pan. Pierce in several places to prevent bubbling and press the tines of a fork around the rim to decorate the crust edge.
3. BAKE for 10 minutes, or until lightly browned.

Campfire Banana Boats

Servings: 4
Cooking Time: 20 Minutes

Ingredients:

- 4 medium, unpeeled ripe bananas
- ¼ cup dark chocolate chips
- 4 teaspoons shredded, unsweetened coconut
- ½ cup mini marshmallows
- 4 graham crackers, chopped

Directions:

1. Preheat the toaster oven to 400°F on BAKE for 5 minutes.
2. Cut the bananas lengthwise through the skin about halfway through. Open the pocket to create a space for the other ingredients.
3. Evenly divide the chocolate, coconut, marshmallows, and graham crackers among the bananas.
4. Tear off four 12-inch squares of foil and place the bananas in the center of each. Crimp the foil around the banana to form a boat.
5. Place the bananas on the baking tray, two at a time, and in position 2, bake for 10 minutes until the fillings are gooey and the banana is warmed through.
6. Repeat with the remaining two bananas and serve.

Make-ahead Chocolate Chip Cookies

Servings: 12

Cooking Time: 45 Minutes

Ingredients:

- 2⅛ cups (10⅔ ounces) all-purpose flour
- ½ teaspoon baking soda
- ½ teaspoon table salt
- 1 cup packed (7 ounces) light brown sugar
- ½ cup (3½ ounces)granulated sugar
- 12 tablespoons unsalted butter, melted and cooled
- 1 large egg plus 1 large yolk
- 2 teaspoons vanilla extract
- 1 cup (6 ounces) semisweet chocolate chips

Directions:

1. Adjust toaster oven rack to middle position and preheat the toaster oven to 350 degrees. Line large and small rimmed baking sheets with parchment paper. Whisk flour, baking soda, and salt together in bowl.

2. Whisk brown sugar and granulated sugar together in medium bowl. Whisk in melted butter until combined. Whisk in egg and yolk and vanilla until smooth. Gently stir in flour mixture with rubber spatula until soft dough forms. Fold in chocolate chips.

3. Working with 2 tablespoons dough at a time, roll into balls. Space desired number of dough balls at least 1½ inches apart on prepared small sheet; space remaining dough balls evenly on prepared large sheet. Using bottom of greased dry measuring cup, press each ball until 2 inches in diameter.

4. Bake small sheet of cookies until edges are just beginning to brown and centers are soft and puffy, 10 to 15 minutes. Let cookies cool slightly on sheet. Serve warm or at room temperature.

5. Freeze remaining large sheet of cookies until firm, about 1 hour. Transfer cookies to 1-gallon zipper-lock bag and freeze for up to 1 month. Bake frozen cookies as directed; do not thaw.

Triple Chocolate Brownies

Servings: 16

Cooking Time: 25 Minutes

Ingredients:

- ⅓ cup salted butter, room temperature, plus extra for greasing the baking dish
- ¾ cup brown sugar
- 2 large eggs
- 1 teaspoon vanilla extract
- ½ cup all-purpose flour
- ¼ cup cocoa powder
- ¼ teaspoon baking powder
- ⅛ teaspoon salt
- ½ cup dark chocolate chips
- ¼ cup white chocolate chips

Directions:

1. Place the rack in position 1 and preheat the oven to 325°F on BAKE for 5 minutes.
2. Lightly grease a 6-inch-square baking dish with butter.
3. In a large bowl, beat together the butter and sugar with an electric hand beater or a whisk until combined. Add the eggs and vanilla and beat to combine.
4. Beat in the flour, cocoa powder, baking powder, and salt until just combined.
5. Stir in dark chocolate and white chocolate chips, then spoon the batter into the prepared dish.
6. Bake for 25 minutes or until a knife inserted in the center comes out mostly clean.
7. Cool in the baking dish and serve.

Hasselback Apple Crisp

Servings: 4

Cooking Time: 20 Minutes

Ingredients:

- 2 large Gala apples, peeled, cored and cut in half
- ¼ cup butter, melted
- ½ teaspoon ground cinnamon
- 2 tablespoons sugar
- Topping
- 3 tablespoons butter, melted
- 2 tablespoons brown sugar
- ¼ cup chopped pecans
- 2 tablespoons rolled oats
- 1 tablespoon flour
- vanilla ice cream
- caramel sauce

Directions:

1. Place the apples cut side down on a cutting board. Slicing from stem end to blossom end, make 8 to 10 slits down the apple halves but only slice three quarters of the way through the apple, not all the way through to the cutting board.

2. Preheat the toaster oven to 330°F and pour a little water into the bottom of the air fryer oven drawer. (This will help prevent the grease that drips into the bottom drawer from burning and smoking.)

3. Transfer the apples to the air fryer oven, flat side down. Combine ¼ cup of melted butter, cinnamon and sugar in a small bowl. Brush this butter mixture onto the apples and air-fry at 330°F for 15 minutes. Baste the apples several times with the butter mixture during the cooking process.

4. While the apples are air-frying, make the filling. Combine 3 tablespoons of melted butter with the brown sugar, pecans, rolled oats and flour in a bowl. Stir with a fork until the mixture resembles small crumbles.

5. When the timer on the air fryer oven is up, spoon the topping down the center of the apples. Air-fry at 330°F for an additional 5 minutes.

6. Transfer the apples to a serving plate and serve with vanilla ice cream and caramel sauce.

Raspberry Hand Pies

Servings: 6

Cooking Time: 20 Minutes

Ingredients:

- 2 cups fresh raspberries
- ¼ cup granulated sugar, plus extra for topping
- 1 tablespoon cornstarch
- 1 tablespoon freshly squeezed lemon juice
- 2 store-bought unbaked pie crusts
- 1 large egg
- 1 tablespoon water
- Oil spray (hand-pumped)

Directions:

1. Preheat the toaster oven to 350°F on AIR FRY for 5 minutes.
2. Place the air-fryer basket in the baking tray.
3. In a medium bowl, stir the raspberries, sugar, cornstarch, and lemon juice until well mixed.
4. Lay the pie crusts on a clean work surface and cut out 6 (6-inch) circles.
5. Evenly divide the raspberry mixture among the circles, placing it in the center.
6. In a small bowl, beat together the egg and water with a fork. Use the egg wash to lightly moisten the edges of the circles, then fold them over to create a half-moon shape. Use a fork to crimp around the rounded part of the pies to seal.
7. Lightly spray the pies with the oil and sprinkle with sugar. Cut 2 to 3 small slits in each pie and place three pies in the basket.
8. In position 2, air fry for 10 minutes until golden brown. Repeat with the remaining pies.
9. Cool the pies and serve.

Cowboy Cookies

Servings: 3

Cooking Time: 14 Minutes

Ingredients:

- Recommended Hamilton Beach® Product: Stand Mixers
- 1 cup butter
- 1 cup sugar
- 1 cup light brown sugar
- 2 eggs
- 2 cups flour
- 1 teaspoon baking soda
- ½ teaspoon baking powder
- ½ teaspoon salt
- 2 cups oatmeal
- 1 tablespoon vanilla
- 12 ounces chocolate chips
- 1 ½ cups coconut

Directions:

1. Preheat the toaster oven to 350°F.

2. With flat beater attachment, cream together butter, sugar, and brown sugar at a medium setting until well blended. Mix in vanilla and eggs. Reduce speed and gradually add flour, baking soda, baking powder, and salt mix until smooth.

3. On a low setting, mix in oatmeal, chocolate chips, and coconut until well mixed. Drop rounded spoon full onto ungreased cookie sheet.

4. Bake on middle rack of oven for 12 to 14 minutes.

Coconut Rice Pudding

Servings: 6

Cooking Time: 55 Minutes

Ingredients:

- ½ cup short-grain brown rice
- Pudding mixture:
- 1 egg, beaten
- 1 tablespoon cornstarch
- ½ cup fat-free half-and-half
- ½ cup chopped raisins
- 1 teaspoon vanilla extract
- ½ teaspoon ground cinnamon
- ½ teaspoon grated nutmeg
- Salt to taste
- ¼ cup shredded sweetened coconut
- Fat-free whipped topping

Directions:

1. Preheat the toaster oven to 400° F.
2. Combine the rice and 1½ cups water in a 1-quart 8½ × 8½ × 4-inch ovenproof baking dish. Cover with aluminum foil.
3. BAKE, covered, for 45 minutes, or until the rice is tender. Remove from the oven and add the pudding mixture ingredients, mixing well.
4. BAKE, uncovered, for 10 minutes, or until the top is lightly browned. Sprinkle the top with coconut and chill before serving. Top with fat-free whipped topping.

Almond Amaretto Bundt Cake

Servings: 8

Cooking Time: 37 Minutes

Ingredients:

- Nonstick baking spray with flour
- 1 (15.25- to 18-ounce) box yellow cake mix
- 1 (3.9-ounce) box vanilla instant pudding
- 1 cup sour cream
- ½ cup canola or vegetable oil
- ¼ cup amaretto or almond liqueur
- 4 large eggs
- ¼ teaspoon pure almond extract
- GLAZE
- 2 ½ cups confectioners' sugar
- 2 tablespoons amaretto
- 1 teaspoon pure vanilla extract
- 1 to 2 tablespoons milk
- Sliced almonds, toasted

Directions:

1. Preheat the toaster oven to 350°F. Spray a 12-cup Bundt pan with nonstick baking spray with flour.

2. Beat the cake mix, instant pudding, sour cream, oil, ¼ cup water, the amaretto, eggs, and almond extract in a large bowl with a handheld mixer at low speed for 30 seconds to combine the ingredients. Scrape the sides of the bowl with a rubber scraper. Beat on medium-high speed for 2 minutes.

3. Pour the batter into the prepared pan. Bake for 30 to 35 minutes, or until a wooden pick inserted into the center comes out clean.

4. Place the pan on a wire rack to cool for 10 minutes. Invert the cake onto the rack and let cool completely.

5. Meanwhile, make the glaze: Whisk the sugar, amaretto, vanilla, and 1 tablespoon milk in a small bowl. If needed, stir in the additional milk to make the desired consistency. Pour over the cake. Garnish with the sliced almonds.

Peach Cobbler

Servings: 4

Cooking Time: 35 Minutes

Ingredients:

- FOR THE FILLING
- 4 cups chopped fresh peaches
- ½ cup sugar
- 2 tablespoons cornstarch
- 1 teaspoon vanilla extract
- FOR THE COBBLER
- 1 cup all-purpose flour
- ¼ cup sugar
- ¾ teaspoon baking powder
- Pinch of sea salt
- 3 tablespoons cold salted butter, cut into ½-inch cubes
- ½ cup buttermilk

Directions:

1. To make the filling
2. In a medium bowl, toss together the peaches, sugar, cornstarch, and vanilla.
3. Transfer to an 8-inch-square baking dish. Set aside.
4. To make the cobbler
5. Place the rack in position 1 and preheat the toaster oven to 350°F on BAKE for 5 minutes.
6. In a large bowl, stir the flour, sugar, baking powder, and sea salt.
7. Using your fingertips, rub the butter into the flour mixture until the mixture resembles coarse crumbs.
8. Add the buttermilk in a thin stream to the flour crumbs, tossing with a fork until a sticky dough forms.
9. Scoop the batter by tablespoons and dollop it on the peaches, spacing the mounds out evenly and leaving gaps for the steam to escape.
10. Bake for 35 minutes, or until the cobbler is golden brown and the filling is bubbly.
11. Serve warm.

Make-ahead Oatmeal-raisin Cookies

Servings: 8

Cooking Time: 45 Minutes

Ingredients:

- 1 cup (5 ounces) all-purpose flour
- ¾ teaspoon table salt
- ½ teaspoon baking soda
- ¼ teaspoon ground cinnamon
- ¾ cup (5¼ ounces) dark brown sugar
- ½ cup (3½ ounces) granulated sugar
- ½ cup vegetable oil
- 4 tablespoons unsalted butter, melted and cooled
- 1 large egg plus 1 large yolk
- 1 teaspoon vanilla extract
- 3 cups (9 ounces) old-fashioned rolled oats
- ½ cup raisins

Directions:

1. Adjust toaster oven rack to middle position and preheat the toaster oven to 350 degrees. Line large and small rimmed baking sheets with parchment paper. Whisk flour, salt, baking soda, and cinnamon together in bowl.

2. Whisk brown sugar and granulated sugar together in medium bowl. Whisk in oil and melted butter until combined. Whisk in egg and yolk and vanilla until smooth. Gently stir in flour mixture with rubber spatula until soft dough forms. Fold in oats and raisins until evenly distributed (mixture will be stiff).

3. Working with 3 tablespoons dough at a time, roll into balls. Space desired number of dough balls at least 1½ inches apart on prepared small sheet; space remaining dough balls evenly on prepared large sheet. Using bottom of greased dry measuring cup, press each ball until 2½ inches in diameter.

4. Bake small sheet of cookies until edges are just beginning to brown and centers are still soft but not wet, 10 to 15 minutes. Let cookies cool slightly on sheet. Serve warm or at room temperature.

5. Freeze remaining large sheet of cookies until firm, about 1 hour. Transfer cookies to 1-gallon zipper-lock bag and freeze for up to 1 month. Bake frozen cookies as directed; do not thaw.

Green Grape Meringues

Servings: 4

Cooking Time: 40 Minutes

Ingredients:

- 1 cup sugar
- 3 egg whites, beaten until stiff
- ½ teaspoon lemon juice
- Vanilla frozen yogurt
- 1 cup sliced fresh green grapes
- 2 squares unsweetened baking chocolate, shaved
- Nonfat whipped topping

Directions:

1. Preheat the toaster oven to 250° F.

2. Add the sugar slowly to the egg white mixture and continue to beat. Add the lemon juice. With a tablespoon, drop on an oiled or nonstick 6½ × 10-inch baking sheet to make a mound of meringue approximately 2 inches across. Make a slight depression in the center of each one.

3. BAKE for 40 minutes, or until crusty and browned. Cool and fill each meringue shell with a scoop of vanilla frozen yogurt. Top with equal portions of green grapes, chocolate shavings, and nonfat whipped topping. The meringues may be stored in an airtight container until ready to use.

Coconut Cake

Servings: 6

Cooking Time: 25 Minutes

Ingredients:

- 2 cups unbleached flour
- 2 teaspoons baking powder
- 1 cup skim or low-fat soy milk
- 2 tablespoons vegetable oil
- 3 1 teaspoon vanilla extract
- 1 egg, beaten
- ¾ cup sugar
- Salt to taste
- Creamy Frosting (recipe follows)

Directions:

1. Preheat the toaster oven to 350° F.

2. Combine all the ingredients in a large bowl, mixing well.

3. Pour the cake batter into an oiled or nonstick 8½ × 8½ × 2-inch square baking (cake) pan.

4. BAKE for 25 minutes, or until a toothpick inserted in the center comes out clean. Ice with Creamy Frosting and sprinkle with coconut.

Chocolate Caramel Pecan Cupcakes

Servings: 6

Cooking Time: 20 Minutes

Ingredients:

- 6 tablespoons all-purpose flour
- 6 tablespoons unsweetened cocoa powder
- ¼ teaspoon baking soda
- ¼ teaspoon baking powder
- ⅛ teaspoon table salt
- 6 tablespoons unsalted butter, softened
- ½ cup granulated sugar
- 1 large egg
- ½ teaspoon pure vanilla extract
- ½ cup sour cream
- BUTTERCREAM FROSTING
- ¼ cup unsalted butter, softened
- 1 ¾ cups confectioners' sugar
- 2 to 3 tablespoons half-and-half or milk
- 1 teaspoon pure vanilla extract
- Caramel ice cream topping
- ¼ cup caramelized chopped pecans

Directions:

1. Preheat the toaster oven to 350°F. Line a 6-cup muffin pan with cupcake papers.

2. Whisk the flour, cocoa, baking soda, baking powder, and salt in a small bowl; set aside.

3. Beat the butter and granulated sugar in a large bowl with a handheld mixer at medium-high speed for 2 minutes, or until the mixture is light and creamy. Beat in the egg well. Beat in the vanilla.

4. On low speed, beat in the flour mixture in thirds, alternating with the sour cream, beginning and ending with the flour mixture. The batter will be thick.

5. Spoon the batter evenly into the prepared cupcake cups, filling each about three-quarters full. Bake for 18 to 20 minutes, or until a wooden pick inserted into the center comes out clean. Place on a wire rack and let cool completely.

6. Meanwhile, make the frosting: Beat the butter in a large bowl using a handheld mixer on medium-high speed until creamy. Gradually beat in the confectioners' sugar. Beat in 2 tablespoons of half-and-half and the vanilla. Beat in the remaining tablespoon of half-and-half, as needed, until the frosting is of desired consistency.

7. Frost each cooled cupcake. Drizzle the caramel topping in thin, decorative stripes over the frosting. Top with the caramelized pecans.

Heavenly Chocolate Cupcakes

Servings: 6

Cooking Time: 30 Minutes

Ingredients:

- 2 squares semisweet chocolate
- 2 tablespoons margarine
- 1 cup unbleached flour
- 2 teaspoons baking powder
- Salt to taste
- ¾ cup brown sugar
- ½ cup skim milk
- 1 egg, beaten
- ½ cup chopped pecans
- ½ teaspoon vanilla extract

Directions:

1. Melt the chocolate and margarine in an oiled or nonstick 8½ × 8½ × 2-inch square baking (cake) pan under the broiler for 5 minutes, or until about half melted. Remove from the oven and stir until completely melted and blended.

2. Combine the flour, baking powder, salt, and sugar in a medium bowl, mixing well. Add the melted chocolate/margarine mixture, then the milk and egg. Stir to blend well, then stir in the pecans and vanilla. Fill paper baking cups or well-oiled tins in a 6-muffin pan three-quarters full with batter.

3. BAKE at 350° F. for 25 minutes, or until a toothpick inserted in the center comes out clean.